DRINK YOUR
TROUBLES AWAY

by JOHN B. LUST

Published and Distributed by
BENEDICT LUST PUBLICATIONS
Box 404 • **New York 10156**

DRINK YOUR TROUBLES AWAY

Beneficial Books are Published by
BENEDICT LUST PUBLICATIONS
NEW YORK, NEW YORK 10156-0404 U.S.A.

This New Expanded Beneficial Book edition has been completely reset in a typeface designed for easy reading, and was printed from new plates. It contains every word from the higher-priced hardcover edition under its original title, The New Raw Juice Therapy.

PRINTING HISTORY
Continuously published since the first
Beneficial Book edition / January 1967
All Rights Reserved
Copyright © 1967 by Benedict Lust Publications
Copyright © 1991 by Benedict Lust Publications
This book may not be reproduced in whole or in part by any means without written permission from the Publisher.

Publisher's Note: *Where any condition has progressed to a serious stage, or if uncertainty exists as to the seriousness, it is best not to delay timely professional services of a competent physician. This book may not be used in any manner to promote the sale of any products mentioned herein.*

ISBN 0-87904-006-8

Library of Congress Catalog Number 66-28198

Printed in the United States Of America

Foreword

by DR. BENEDICT LUST

Since the earliest ages, Medical Science has been of all sciences the most unscientific. It has sought to cure disease by the magic of pills, potions and poisons that surpress the symptoms rather than attack the real cause of the ailment. It has always believed in the superstition that the use of chemical substances, which are in themselves harmful and destructive to human life, will prove an efficient antidote for the violation of natural laws. In this way, it has encouraged man to go the limit in self-indulgence, weakening and destroying his physical system, in the expectation that by simply swallowing a few pills or submitting to an injection of serum or vaccine he will be absolved of any ill effects arising from his bad living habits.

From the earliest to the present time, medical hucksters have found it ten times easier to relieve a man of ten dollars by acting on his superstition than extracting one dollar from him by appealing to his reason and common sense. With this key to a gold mine in their pocket, the apostles of "orthodox" medicine have indulged in the most blatantly outrageous and unscientific methods of curing disease because these have been in keeping with their medical prestige.

Away back in primitive times, disease was regarded as a demon to be exorcised from its victim. The medicine man belabored the body of his patient with a bag, rattling with bones and feathers. No doubt in extreme cases the tremendous faith held by the patient in this method of cure really proved effective. But for this mental science should be thanked—not the bag of bones and feathers.

Coming down to the middle ages, the Witches' Broth—one ingredient of which was the blood of a child murderer drawn in the dark of the moon—was the vogue. Official medicine regarded it as a remedy for every disease.

In a later period, the *docteur a la mode*, between his pinches of snuff, would order his victim bled as a remedy for what he called spirits, vapors, humours, megrims or miasms. These names were eventually replaced by full-blown Greek and Latin names—equally as meaningless.

Following this pseudo-scientific diagnosis and treatment came the drugging phase. The symptoms of the disease were attacked unmercifully by all kinds of drugs, alkalis, acids and poisons which, by suppressing the symptoms, were supposed to enhance the vitality of the patient. All these cures have had their period of inception and extensive application—and, fortunately, of certain disuse. Today the popularity of the serums and antibiotics is at its peak. These, instead of being an improvement on the "medicines" of former times, on the contrary, introduce further toxins in the body, often with most distressing and deadly effects.

The policy of expediency is at the basis of medical drug healing. It is along the lines of self-indulgence, indifference, ignorance and lack of self-control that drug medicine lives. Mankind is exploited by a system of medicine, founded on poisonous and revolting products, whose chemical composition and mode of attack are both equally unknown to their originators. This is called "scientific medicine."

The *natural* system for curing disease, on the other hand, is based on a return to Nature in regulating the diet, breathing, exercising, bathing and the employment of various other *natural* forces to eliminate the poisonous substances in the system and so raise the vitality and health of the patient.

Official medicine has at all times attacked the symptoms of disease paying very little attention to its causes. Natural medicine is concerned far more with removing the causes of disease than merely curing its symptoms.

Natural healing is the most desirable factor in the regeneration of the race. It is a return to nature in methods of living and treatment. It makes use of the elementary forces of Nature, of chemical selection of foods that will constitute a correct medical dietary.

There is really but one healing force in existence and that is Nature herself: that is, the inherent restorative power of the organism to overcome disease. Now the question is, how can this power be guided more readily and appropriately? By the irritating drugs, serums and vaccines used by superstitious moderns or by the bland, congenial forces of Natural Therapeutics? Are not these natural forces much more orthodox than the artificial resources of the druggist? The practical application of these natural agencies, duly suited to the individual case are the true signs and whole art of healing.

Table of Contents

Drink Your Troubles Away

Preface to the Revised Edition

It has been said that every seven years your body completely renews itself. Something along those lines has happened to this book. The previous edition held great promise. So, that text of the book has been fully retained and new material has been added. Naturally, technological advancements have been recognized and these have made necessary the revision of the chapter on juicing machines. A glossary and supplementary chapter have been added to include scientific evidence supporting what *Raw Juice Therapy* promised eight years ago.

All together, we have now what I believe is a *transcendental* work. Anything transcendental, or enduring, whether it is a painting, a sculpture, a poem or a play, must possess three qualities: beauty, truth and goodness. These qualities permeate this book's subject, nature's radiant fruits and glorious vegetables. Their beauty is in a floral form, colors that evade the greatest artists, shapes that please the eye and fragrances that stimulate the senses. Their truth lies in their innocent simplicity, nature's unadulterated gift of vitality to man through these living foods and their goodness is in their harmonious effect on man's health which you can notice by his clear skin, sparkling eyes and vigor.

And now, in the hope that you will accept this new edition in the spirit in which I present it to you, I offer you *Drink Your Troubles Away.*

J.B.L.
New Canaan, Conn.

THAT WONDERFUL BODY OF YOURS

No human mind can fully comprehend, in its entirety, the living processes going on unceasingly inside the body throughout an entire lifetime. Your body may be compared to a machine through which you "connect up" with the world around you. It is the most useful and valuable possession you will ever have.

Man has beaten the so-called laws of "The Impossible". He has gone up in the air to heights in space where birds cannot reach. He has gone under water, staying for weeks without coming up for air, beating the birds and fish at their own game. There is not a savage beast that he cannot tame and master. Man, as he stands today, holds the system of power externally. He has gone into Nature and has harnessed her and he has said, "work". He issues the orders and the world obeys, but he is losing it all by his own weakness or ignorance and indifference toward Nature's laws of health. He has become a slave to disease.

Your efficiency, ability, earning power and capabilities depend almost entirely upon the health of your physical body. How much would you not give for just another twelve months of health and happiness, if you were sure you were to die tomorrow? Good health turns all surroundings of gloom and despair into an atmosphere of happiness and enjoyment. Your body is the finest piece of property you will ever possess; cultivate it, improve it, and guard it.

No culture, education, good breeding or heritage can make us happy without good health. All we possess diminishes in direct proportion as we become sick. Yet, in spite of all these facts, most of you are daily neglecting, injuring, or abusing your body. If you neglect your body ignorantly or willfully you must pay to the last rattle in your throat. Nature never forgives nor excuses for transgressing or disobeying her never-changing, iron laws. Your body is a machine through which you "connect up" with the external world. It is the most useful possession you will ever have, and it is all your own. Unconsciously we view the human body from the outside, giving little or no thought to the intricacy and complexity of the working going on within. We observe the kind of clothing, color of the eyes, styling of the hair, etc., with intense interest but seldom consider the wonders and mysteries of the activities going on within.

No human mind can fully comprehend, in its entirety, the living processes going on unceasingly inside the body throughout an entire lifetime. These functions and activities are infinite and cannot be thoroughly understood by the mind of man. Only Nature can understand.

Watch one of the little red cells in the blood stream — the precision and accuracy in the performance of his task, under the never-erring guidance of the body-intelligence. Floating along in the blood channel with millions of other red cells and corpuscles until it reaches the lungs. There this little fellow grabs up a load of oxygen that has been breathed in, and starts on his journey crowding and dodging around the other fellow workers in the blood stream, some carrying body refuse for elimination, others loaded with deadly carbon-dioxide gas, still others with loads of food for body-building and replacement. Yet with never an error or a mistake, this little red fellow never falters until he has reached the foot and unloaded his oxygen in the tissue cell, and finished the task. It all sounds like a fairy-tale or dream, yet it is as true and real as the rising of the sun, or the beating of your heart.

When you realize that more than fifteen million red blood cells are being produced every minute and poured into your blood stream, you can only stand in awe and amazement. Yet scientific research has proven this to be true. We are told that if every nerve in the human body were placed end to end, they would extend more than two thousand miles in length.

You do not question the supreme control of your body by this inborn intelligence that pumps or transmits life-giving power to every cell, tissue, and organ in your body, from your brain reservoir. There is not a cell or body-organ that has any lifepower to function within itself, but only to serve the body as function-machines essential in carrying on the process of life. For example, your eyes do not see, nor your ears hear; but this body-intelligence sees and hears *through* these function-machines, which record the vibrations of vision and sound. Likewise your stomach does not digest food any more than the hammer drives the nail. It is merely the function-machine *through* which the function of digestion takes place, provided the activating or functioning power freely flowing over the nerve channels that connect your brain-reservoir with the digestive stomach-machine.

The fact that a ripe apple on the table, producing vibrations of sight which reach the intelligence headquarters located in the brain, through the eyes, will start the flowing of stomach juices, proves beyond a doubt the supreme control of the body by the brain.

In view of these facts it is evident, instead of the many chemical elements found in your body producing intelligent life and motion, that it is this inborn, life-giving intelligence which produces energy thereby secreting body-chemicals as a by-product resulting therefrom. This being true, when a condition of perverted or unbalanced chemistry is present in the body, instead of supplying drugs or chemicals, supply *more life* from the brain or life-reservoir to the functioning organ, and the chemicals will then be corrected and supplied from within. Providing, of course, that the right kind of raw elements, or foods are taken into the body for this innate intelligence to act upon and obtain the chemical elements needed. In other words this body intelligence is circumscribed by limitations, though functioning one hundred percent. Those limitations mark the impossibility of producing chemicals from nothing. Organic chemical elements that are present in the living organism are obtained from food material that contain them, and nowhere else. How important then should be our selection of food, to supply these chemicals proportionately.

1. The Theory of Raw Juice Therapy

*I*N NATURE's scheme of things there are pure liquids locked in the cells of plants that have definite therapeutic value. Just as we know that certain herbs have specific curative power, so do these plant juices which come from fresh fruits and vegetables. These juices, subtle in their action, yet more potent than any medicine, and without the toxic effect of drugs, can eliminate or prevent many of the chronic and degenerative diseases with which human beings are afflicted.

Fresh fruit juices are the *cleansers* of the human system. Vegetable juices are the *regenerators* and *builders* of the body. Grown in healthy soil, they contain all the substances needed for nourishing the human organism, provided the juices are used fresh, raw and without preservatives. The substances may all be grouped into seven simple kinds of materials. These are (1) Carbohydrates, (2) Proteins, (3) Fats, (4) Minerals, (5) Vitamins, (6) Bio Flavonoids and (7) Cellulose.

1

I propose to show in this book the effects of fresh fruit and vegetable juices upon the body. The various types of mechanical appliances for juicing fruits and vegetables will be discussed, pointing out the advantages and disadvantages of each. The choice of which one best meets your individual requirements will be left up to you.

Scientists tell us that many diseases are the results of a diet deficient in trace vitamins and organic materials. Specifically such diseases as pellagra, beri beri, rickets, malnutrition, anemia, the conditions of underweight, overweight and even the common cold and vague virus disorders can be traced to a lack of these life-giving units of health. Fresh vegetable juices satisfy and nourish every one of the twenty-six thousand billion cells of which our bodies are composed. They revitalize the blood stream. They revivify the nerves. They rejuvenate the glands and organs. They soothe the acid-irritated tissues.

When we consider that vegetables and fruits have been naturally cooked by solar energy; that they contain all the elements the sun and the earth have buried deep in their fibre cells; that they are nature's live-cell foods—then it follows as logical that if we crush the juices from the cells of these fresh fruits and vegetables and put their health giving fluid into our blood stream, we will receive a share of their vital energy. Raw juices, properly extracted, are second only to raw honey in ease and speed of assimilation. Raw juices taken on an empty stomach will be absorbed by the blood stream and glands within 15 minutes after ingestion. This vital part of vegetables is most difficult to reach. It is secreted within the cellulose fibres we call "roughage." While roughage is definitely something we want included in our daily meals, it is possible to get too much of it. Therefore, and because we are seeking the effect of the pure plant juices without taxing our systems with roughage, raw juices provide the answer to so many health problems that have a nutritional solution.

The good quality electric juicing machines will extract fully the vital nutritive elements from fruits and vegetables. Drinking the juices from which most of the pulp has not been separated taxes the digestive organs more than eating and properly masticating the whole raw fruits or vegetables themselves. This is so because the roughage thus taken into the stomach has been thoroughly insalivated in the mouth during the chewing process and it is here where digestion begins.

We know that fresh fruits and vegetables contain vitamins and minerals essential to good health, to the prolongation of life, and to the cure of disease. We know also that a certain amount of these vitamins and minerals are destroyed in the cooking of foods, so we conclude that they are best consumed raw.

Because we can only consume a limited amount of raw food daily, generally not enough to obtain the therapeutic effect desired, a pint or more of fresh raw fruit or vegetable juice added to the diet of the average person will do more than is popularly realized.

Here we must make note that the cure of disease is a long, slow process. If a person in ill health thinks that by adding a pint or two of fresh juices to his daily diet, he will be in perfect health in a few days, he is mistaken.

While an improvement in the general vitality may be noted after a week or two, it takes a long time for its full cure to develop. Nature works slowly but efficiently. It takes 20 years to build a baby into a man. With patience you'll discover that many stubborn physical ailments will respond to long range planned raw juice therapy.

Basically, it is intended to correct the colloidal cell chemical composition which has become unbalanced through the unnatural daily living and dieting habits we literally are forced into accepting. It is easy to understand that the commonly accepted practice of trying to suppress the symptoms arising from living like this is more harmful than helpful.

For the person who is ill, there are various combinations of juices in prescribed quantities as outlined in the chapter about specific diseases.

You must bear in mind that where a person's condition has progressed to a serious stage, or if uncertainty exists as to seriousness, it is best not to delay the timely competent services of a physician. But, in the regeneration and reconstruction of your body by raw juice therapy, it is important to remember also that these juices will start a detoxifying process throughout your entire system. Eliminative processes thus begun are sometimes very powerful, having the force to dissolve and expel hardened and caked masses which have lodged in various locations throughout the body and its glandular system during the long period when these encumbrances were being accumulated. These impurities cannot withstand the avalanche of sudden and overwhelming ingestion of vegetable juices and under their repeated impact, deposits or 'encumbrances' as Louis Kuhne, author of *The New Science of Healing* termed toxic accumulations, are reabsorbed by the blood stream and cast out. As the blood becomes more alkaline, the toxins which have been built up in the tissues through years of wrong living are dissolved and enter again into the circulation of the blood stream to be carried off via the regular excretory channels. This is the original naturopathic theory of a "single cause for all disease." It is interesting to note that some of the most exciting results of current scientific medical research are leading to the conclusion that man does not reach the normal span of life that Nature awards all living things because of tiny toxic substances deposited in the cells of our tissues, gradually causing them to lose their elasticity and functional power. Think what this means when any one of your organ's tissues are involved. The cause of trouble always seems so mystifying until the "unity of disease" theory is applied.

But, to return to the "healing crisis," we must not become unduly alarmed over the discomforts occurring during it. Those of you who have for years lived on highly seasoned foods, abundant proteins, pastries and heavy starches, will almost invariably complain of distress when starting a rigorous raw juice schedule. Such disagreeable reactions do not mean that raw juices do not agree with you, but signify they do not harmonize with an unhealthy condition of the stomach and bowels or an acid condition of the blood. That is why these unpleasant symptoms must not be misinterpreted as a change for the worse, when they are really signs of improvement. It seems not only unscientific, but positively unreasonable to expect good wholesome raw fruit or vegetable juice to combine with sickly secretions in the same manner and with the same effect as they do with normal secretions. All corrections, and they begin promptly, must of necessity be accompanied by some discomfort and distress until the effective uprooting of the bodily poisons has been achieved.

Our bodies are made of the material that goes into them, food, air and the magnetic forces of Nature about us. All of these factors are fairly constant except food. We are, therefore, essentially made of the things we eat. We reflect very quickly the food that we consume. What goes into our bodies today forms blood, flesh and bones tomorrow.

Now the question arises, "What is the most perfect food?." The answer is, "Food as it grows." As Nature prepared it in her own laboratory it has been as perfectly made as is possible under any circumstance.

Therefore raw juice therapy answers our need completely for making food available to us in its most natural originally live state in order that it can most perfectly sustain life.

The difficulty in proving this contention lies in the confusing results that occur when a sick, imperfect body is given the most perfect food, raw plant juices. Living, vital, perfect food will first cast out the old, dying, decaying imperfections within, as you know. The organism can be built only when the decaying materials are removed and a new structure is built upon a solid, clean foundation.

The removal of these toxic substances through eruptions, fevers, inflammations, headaches and diarrhea means internal disturbances, biological reactions (ordinarily called diseases) which temporarily cause discomfort and discouragement when not properly understood. Each such reaction, properly treated, leaves the organism in better condition, more vital than before, after it is over. Results of natural food dieting can only bring about radiant health and freedom from disease.

An interesting case history of a raw juice cure was the case of Mr. P. O'-, of Milwaukee, Wisconsin, now 61. At the age of 25 he began suffering from a "bladder disease." By the age of 40 he had constant bladder symptoms of pain, burning, frequent urination, bleeding, etc., which became unbearable. He resorted to the usual symptom-suppressing drug procedure with the usual undesirable results. Surgery was finally advised as the only way out. Diagnosis of prostatic tumor, possibly cancerous, was made. At 50, in desperation, he had decided to take his life. Accidentally, at this moment of despair, he learned of raw juice therapy. He read the statement that the ideal diet of man was the raw food diet. Raw juices appealed to his intelligence as an efficient method of obtaining these benefits. Especially so in his particular case because extreme pyorrhea had developed. Hot, moist packs were applied to his teeth and the bladder area. After a three day fast he was started on mixed juices of apples, oranges, spinach, carrots, beets, celery, cucumber and parsley. He soon began to feel some relief and gained courage. From the age of 51 to 52 he gradually restricted his solid foods to raw fruits and vegetables too. He resorted to a mild herbal laxative to relieve the severe constipation from which he was suffering. From 52 to 53 he suffered extreme hunger, eating continually during the day and sometimes at night. During this time he had copious eliminations from all organs of elimination, including the skin. He had a sickly yellow, jaundiced color. Odors emanating from his body were so extreme that relatives and friends shunned him. Starting at 160 lb. weight, he came down to "skin and bones." All the while he felt miserable from the continuous eliminations. Then, quite suddenly, at the age of 53, his appetite normalized, his weight came up to normal for his structure, between 135 and 140 lb., and he began to have more days of feeling in high spirits with a sense of well being he never before experienced. From that time on there has been a gradual rebuilding of all organs and structures with an ever-increasing reserve of strength and endurance. Firm muscles replace flabby ones. The prostatic and bladder conditions have cleared up completely. Each year his resistance to colds grows stronger.

He relishes his raw juices and raw foods more as time goes on.

Today most of us are familiar with the subject of vitamins and minerals. We know that vitamins and minerals are not foods in themselves; they are organic substances present in the foods we eat. That is, food we eat that has not been tampered with. Cooking and modern refining and preserving processes destroy these valuable substances. Vitamins do not furnish energy itself, but are essential for transforming food into energy. They also serve as regulators to your body processes. A lack of vitamins or minerals in your body means that you have little or no protection against disease. You will not enjoy maximum good health; in fact, your health may be seriously damaged.

For an example that leaves no doubt in anyone's mind about the certainty of what can happen from a vitamin or mineral deficiency we have the true story of the battleship "KRONPRINZ WILHELM" which sailed into the Navy base at Newport News in April 1915 with 110 of her crew of 500 completely disabled with paralysis of limbs, shrivelled muscles, dilated hearts, anemia, edema, and painful neuritis, and with further similar casualties dropping at the rate of two a day. The ship had scouted the seas for 255 successive days without touching port, sinking her enemies' ships and stocking herself with looted provisions "being able to give each member of her crew as much as three pounds of meat a day for an entire year." Her larder was stocked with plenty of butter, biscuits, potatoes, ham, bacon, beans, tea, coffee, milk, margarine, pastries, salt fish, wines, beer, whisky and other so-called luxuries. Truly her crew lived on "the fat of the land"—but without the faintest trace of a fresh fruit or vegetable in the whole set-up. The result was casualty after casualty almost to the point of surrender. They were saved in a last-minute rescue—by an enlightened doctor who prescribed a diet which amounted, in general, to little more than a hot water infusion of whole, natural foods, containing the dissolved-out mineral salts, which was fed to the men as soup. Typical of the doctor's prescription was one which directed: "Wash and peel potatoes. Throw away the potatoes and retain the skins. Boil the skins and give the liquid to the men to drink—4 ounces a day."

This dietary regime was begun on April 16th and in ten days, 47 of the sick men were so far improved that the ship's doctor reported, "We can safely say they are cured." One man whose limbs had been completely paralyzed was able to stand without help. Before long the entire crew had regained their health and were ready to go to sea again. This example emphasizes dramatically how important vitamins and minerals are to the human system.

So it has been known for a good many years that minerals are an essential part of anyone's daily intake, but it is too often forgotten until some dramatic event takes place which proves the contention all over again. In an age of startling medical experiments, perhaps one of the most dramatic centered around this very question of mineral deficiency.

Twelve prisoners—all serving long terms—were offered an unconditional pardon if they would submit to living a few weeks on a diet which entirely excluded minerals. The men, naturally enough, welcomed this opportunity for freedom and felt it would be an easy way out of their troubles.

They soon found out differently. Originally, the experiment was scheduled to last for sixty days. After only a few days, the men refused to continue even though they knew a pardon awaited them.

Some tried to commit suicide because they were suffering so greatly. Six of them developed pellagra—that creeping death which results from diet deficiencies—and two others showed definite signs of the disease.

Newspapers all over the country carried the story on their front pages. Protests over the inhuman treatment came from all parts of the nation. Finally the government had to bow to public opinion. But, this is the most dramatic part of the whole story. The men were put on high mineral rations, and without exception all of them were restored to complete health.

These two stories ought to be all the proof needed that minerals must be a regular part of your diet. Many people consider sickness something that is inflicted upon them, something which they are powerless to prevent. Nothing could be further from the truth.

When you become ill, it is simply a sign that you have not been living the way Nature intended you to live. One of the greatest drawbacks to regaining health is the attitude of someone suffering from ailments or disease. Because of your lowered vitality it is easy to let discouragement overtake you. It takes time to rebuild your body, to rid it of the poisons which you have allowed to accumulate, to restore those elements of which you have been starved.

Many people, at such a time, allow themselves to be persuaded to have unnecessary surgery performed. They even try one so-called 'cure' after another in the hopes of an overnight miracle. There is, however, only one miracle and that is Nature's curative power—if you live in such a way that Nature has an opportunity to work her miracle.

Health can be regained only if you feed your body the minerals and vitamins of which it has been deprived. There is no better way to do this than the simple regime of raw juice therapy. I would like to add one word of caution, though. Your mental attitude must be a hopeful one, and you must avoid worry. Culivating the art of relaxation will do wonders to speed your recovery.

Remember: The body is *consuming* energy when tense and is *restoring* energy when it is relaxed. Our everyday life naturally calls for the use of energy; everything we do is a call on our reserves of energy. If at the same time you are tense and worried, there is a further drain on your energy. Worry can bring on fatigue almost quicker than anything else. So do not worry about your health. Do what is necessary to rebuild it, but do not dwell upon it.

Raw vegetable juices are the perfect food for both elderly people and those who have become ill through faulty living habits. Many of these people find it almost impossible to eat enough of the natural foods they need because the entire length of their alimentary canal is in such poor condition that they cannot properly utilize such foods. The raw juices will supply concentrated and easily assimilable amounts of vitamins and minerals. Furthermore, it's nearly impossible to take too much of them for the normal hunger mechanism of each one will naturally tend to govern their intake. Besides, with the exception of vitamin A and D, vitamins and minerals when taken in over-abundance can be stored or carried away as wastes without harm to the body. This is not true of other foods.

It's also interesting to note that it's very nearly impossible to overeat when the diet is adequately supplied with vitamins and minerals. There is simply no desire to do so. Raw juice therapy is thus in complete keeping with the healthful "harmony-with-Nature" concept of living.

Every acute disease is not destructive,
not an enemy to be dreaded,
but a friend and helper if properly treated.
This conception . . . explains and justifies
the Biblical injunctions,
"Resist not evil, but overcome evil with good."

Dr. Henry Lindlahr

2. An Antidote for Our Daily Poison

*R*AW JUICE THERAPY is a Natural, drugless therapy proven by years of scientific research. It was established many years ago that people were literally starving because of vitamin and mineral deficiencies even though they were eating heavy "meat and potato" meals every day. Although this was known, and a sturdy band of diet reform pioneers tried hard to convince a credulous public that their eating habits were shortening their lives, decades went by before clinical tests provided evidence that certain deficiencies of food elements caused specific diseases. Finally when the laws of food chemistry were definitely established it became possible to diagnose the various ailments and to determine just which vitamins and minerals were necessary to overcome the different disabilities.

In a day and age of devitalized foods it is especially important to know the laws of proper diet. All too many of us have created grave and serious bodily deficiences by neglecting the laws of Nature. So long as people continue to eat foods that have been prepared of impoverished, ghostly white flour, bleached and sulphured foods, doped and adulterated foods, plaster-like preparations called "breakfast cereals;" so long as they live on inferior food material that has been dyed, chemically treated, doctored up so that it will look and feel fresh for long after it should have spoiled; so long as they live closer to the can opener than to Mother Nature, closer to the baker and the confectioner than to the farmer, closer to the food manufacturer than to the Almighty, closer to the butcher than to the garden and orchard, closer to the drug store than to the health food store, closer to the surgeon than to common sense; so long as they try to live on poisoned, over-heated preserves, scorched, pressure-cooked, fried foods, food that has been altered in its chemistry, disorganized in its molecules by pasteurization, food that has been artificially treated and sulphured until the food juices, vitamins, minerals and other food properties have passed up into the blue sky and there is nothing left but a dessicated, lifeless substance sold as food in every grocery store and super market in the land and eaten by every man, woman and child, including the doctors, and passed upon as meriting seals of approval by various "scientific" organizations; so long as they mill off, peel off, cut off, pare off and cook away from 5 to 16 chemical food elements in the food and eat only the ghostlike starch, food sugar and food fat; so long as they eat food that has stood on warehouse floors and shelves for long periods of time in grime, dirt, dust, heat, moisture and atmospheric ferments, until the food properties have been injured by decomposition, toxins, age, vermin, rodents, metallic contamination and by other agents of decay and corruption; so long as they drink bottled goods, soda fountain pop, artificial fruit drinks that have not a drop of fruit juice in them, laboratory fruit juices that contain powdered dope, dyestuffs, preservatives and glucose; so long as they eat cold storage meat that may have been put in storage when the market price was low and kept for months or even years and doped, doctored and embalmed to be sold when the market price was high; so long as they drink chocolate, cocoa, coffee and tea or eat cream puffs and grease-filled doughnuts and crullers; so long as they eat decomposed, rancid, lifeless, adulterated, fumigated, corrupt foodless food material; so long as they eat fritters, fudge, syrup, soda crackers, cookies, candy, creamless ice cream, starchy noodles, pickled food, pigs' feet, puddings and all such meals of demineralized and devitalized food products presented by the food manufacturers and technicians more interested in how their wares will perform in their assembly-line food processing machines than what their ware will do to your stomach; so long as they continue to procrastinate and postpone obtaining the flood of health that can be released to them through the daily use of Nature's fresh vibrant and vital plant juices; that long will they continue to be half alive and sick, that long will undertakers be in demand early in life, that long will they continue to sacrifice long before its time the greatest miracle of the universe—human life.

The function of food is simply to give us energy, to build our tissues and to regulate our body processes. For this reason, it is essential that we select the right foods—those substances which will do the most for us. Emphasizing the importance of correct selection is this quotation from the famous Dr. Alexis Carrell, long time head of the Rockefeller Institute. He said "Unless the doctors of today become the dieticians of tomorrow, the dieticians of today will become the doctors of tomorrow."

Your blood is your life stream. Health cannot be purchased in drugs, but youth, life and beauty are in good blood. Good blood cannot be made of white bread, embalmed beef, sausage, potatoes, gravy, doughnuts, pie, cake and coffee. Neither can vigor, health, youthfulness and efficiency be maintained on such a diet or even on the conventional "reformed" diet. Health and genius crave and require natural food for the production of good red blood. Disease and failure are the results of a wrong diet. Wrong diet brings with it constipated bowels, hemorrhoids, anemia, defective secretions, acidity, ulcers, bloating, arthritis, headache, nervousness, stomach trouble, liver and kidney ailments, heart disease, feeble-mindedness and thousands of other ailments that have been translated into Greek and Latin, but have never been cured— by the orthodox methods.

The juices of raw fruits and vegetables—freshly extracted—are the richest sources of vitamins and minerals with their trace elements, that can be found. These are Nature's own foods, too often neglected in favor of the diets described above. Fruit and vegetable juices, taken in the correct proportions, will do much to cut down the desire for manufactured foods and meat. And it will do it without any strain on the system and without the troublesome effects of meat.

Eating meat is extravagant. We are getting natural

nourishment at second hand. The fruits and vegetables produce all the protein we need. Then why not take it directly from Nature?

When Nature's food is predigested by animals and then consumed by us, it has aftereffects. In the colon, meat decomposes rapidly and gives rise to acids and toxins which are absorbed into the blood and distributed throughout the entire body. Meat is toxic to the nervous system and throws an unnecessary and harmful burden on the kidneys and liver.

Many people mistakenly think that meat is a great strengthener. It is simple to explode this erroneous theory. It comes primarily from the stimulating effect which meat has on the body. Actually, what happens is that the body is so overstimulated that the excitement is mistaken for strength. Temporarily, a person feels 'strong' although the effect does not last very long. In the end, it really robs the body of strength. It is a form of living on credit. The body overworks and then, through the years of harmful dieting, its reserves are gradually thrown away. How much better it is to choose those foods which actually give strength without any of the harmful aftereffects.

The proper use of raw fruit and vegetable juices will not only restore your health but they will act as a shield against those foods which you should not be eating. You will find that your desire for them — once you have learned the life-giving principle of raw juice therapy—has completely disappeared.

In case you are not certain which are the most dangerous foods, let me say that next to meat, they are the foods which have been artificially preserved. Let us quickly run down the list of these contaminated foods;

Sulphites are regularly mixed with beer and other beverages. They are used by butchers to keep meat from "spoiling." Brightly colored dried apricots and some canned fruits and raisins are bleached with sulphurous acid. The gelatin with which salads are made is sometimes treated with it.

Polished rice is covered with French chalk. Flour is devitaminized, gassed, bleached and often contains some of the acid phosphates. Boric acid or borax and poisonous alkalis are found in bacon and sausage. These are only a few examples, but each of them spells danger to you.

Raw fruit and vegetable juices can not only overcome the desire for these harmful foods, but they can overcome their effect. To quote a famous English doctor, "There is but one cause of disease—poison, toxemia, most of which is created in the body by faulty living habits and faulty elimination." Raw fruit and vegetable juices make it possible to flood the system with the materials which wash away these poisons. Their alkaline minerals loosen the acid poisons which can then be eliminated through the various organs.

New blood cells are born every fourteen days. Vegetable juices can help make the new cells healthier than the old ones. They can build a disease-resisting body. They must be present, though, in the right proportions. That is what is wrong with many of the commercial preparations which are now on the market. They concentrate on one or another of the vitamins or minerals. What is more, they often contain dangerous preservatives. Only raw fruits and vegetables can give you the elements necessary for healthful living. These you can get best by preparing your own juices fresh each time you need them.

Many questions are asked about the direct effect of fruit and vegetable juices on certain diseases. This will be taken up in detail later in this book. I would like, though to tell you some of the effects right now so that you can see for yourself why these juices can accomplish so-called miracles.

Believers in Nature's ways of life and methods of healing have long been aware of the curative powers locked in the yellow or yellowish fruits and vegetables—particularly the citrus fruits such as the orange and lemon.

In recent years the research scientist with his electronic microscope and centrifuge has isolated an incredible variety of healing agents from these aristocrats of Nature's foods, far more than were previously suspected. He has found out what they are—at least some of them—and what they do within the human body. They have been administered in carefully controlled quantities and combinations to the victims of a considerable assortment of ills and diseases. And all along the line the person who tries to live as naturally as possible has been proven right, even to his point of eating as much as possible of the whole fruit or vegetable—including the pulp and even the rind—whenever it is edible.

This is the story of science's latest knowledge of the bioflavonoids and their influence in health and disease. It is highly dramatic and encouraging, particularly to those who are getting along in years, but also to anticipatory mothers and even to the unborn.

What are bioflavonoids? The word is not so formidable as it looks. "Bio," of course, means merely a substance that is active rather than inert in the body's chemistry. "Flavonoid" stems from flavone, a crystalline substance that produces the color yellow in plant life. Thus the bioflavonoids influence our life processes greatly and tend to color certain of our foods yellow. Oranges and lemons contain the greatest concentrations of bioflavonoids, but they are also found in a wide variety of other fruits and vegetables, such as all the citrus fruits, peppers, cabbage, tomatoes, strawberries, watermelon, and numerous others.

The principal bioflavonoids so far discovered include several types of Vitamin C, Vitamin K, Vitamin P, ascorbic acid (once believed to be the entire Vitamin C complex) and hesperidin (a crystalline substance that is largely concentrated in the peel and pulp).

It is not necessary to go into the complex arrangement of the bioflavonoids in the citrus fruits other than to point out the great importance of not only drinking the juices in considerable quantity but of also eating the pulpy flesh. Now for some of the recently proven effects of these bioflavonoids in carefully controlled experiments:

Among other ailments, the bioflavonoids have been proven effective in the treatment of hemorrhagic purpura (skin hemorrhage), other disorders of the capillaries and small blood vessels, pleurisy, tuberculosis, Graves' disease, beriberi, the tendency to habitual abortion, a wide variety of rheumatic ills, certain glandular disturbances, and even the common cold.

It has been remarked that no man is older than his arteries and since this is profoundly true then it is obvious that no man is older than his capillaries. The combined length of a person's capillaries has been estimated as two and one-half times the distance around the globe, which gives some idea of their minuteness. Now it has been proven that the bioflavonoids improve the permeability and strength of the capillary walls, increasing the efficiency of the capillaries in transmitting life-giving ingredients from the blood stream to the cells and removing toxic wastes. From this, the importance of the bioflavonoids in the treatment of such an ailment as rheumatoid arthritis, for example, becomes plain.

Modern thinking, in fact, goes so far as to postulate that any improvement in the condition of the "capillary tree"—as this vast network of tiny vessels is called—will improve the body's ability to fight any and all diseases, while there is no disease condition that does not adversely affect the capillaries.

It has long been recognized, of course, that scurvy was characterized by skin hemorrhages and that it was cured by fresh vegetables and, in particular, citrus fruits. It long bore the name *purpura nautica* or "sailor's purpura" because it was most severe among sailors who were deprived of fresh fruits and vegetables for long months at a time. Shipmasters used to conduct weekly "skin inspections" for the bleeding that warned of the dread disease.

However, scurvy was also widely prevalent on land, becoming more severe in the winter months and in years when vegetable and fruit harvests were poor. We have known for some time the importance of fruits and vegetables in preventing scurvy, but their importance in combatting the rheumatoid ailments is far less appreciated.

It is now established that abnormally fragile capillaries are found frequently in victims of rheumatoid arthritis.

A nutritional breakdown is present, which prevents the sufferers from getting the full benefit from ingested Vitamin C. Striking improvement was shown in patients who were given not only Vitamin C—concentrated in citrus fruit juice—but also hesperidin—which is more prevalent in the peels. The researchers concluded that the hesperidin aided the body in retaining and absorbing Vitamin C, which in turn improved capillary resistance.

The bioflavonoids are now proving of immense value in the handling of ailments once associated inseparably with aging. For example, in the study a group of elderly patients was chosen all of whom were prone to frequent slight hemorrhages of the cerebral blood vessels. Over a period of five years they were given a diet rich in hesperidin and Vitamin C. Both the frequency and the severity of hemorrhages were reduced significantly.

In atherosclerosis, a blood vessel disease commonly associated with the elderly, the vessel walls lose some of their permeability with the result that nutrients fail to get through and malnutrition develops. Again, the bioflavonoid group—including ascorbic acid plus added calcium—appear to improve the condition of the patients, although this research is very new. Actually, they appear to have the capacity of either increasing or decreasing the permeability of the vessels as needed, thus serving as self-regulating controls when the body is functioning with fair efficiency and adequate amounts of all the bioflavonoids are ingested.

Many wives with a tendency to habitual abortion have fragile capillaries, recent research reveals. Even in normal pregnancies there is a tendency toward the increased retention of fluids and edema caused by the passage of fluids through the capillary walls into the spaces between the cells. Vitamins C, K, and P—all found in citrus fruits—have been proven of great value in reducing these conditions. For this purpose, the National Research Council recently recommended that pregnant women consume eight ounces of orange juice daily. Some authorities hold that lemon juice is even more effective; the substance citrin, which heals vascular purpura, has been isolated from it. In addition, frequent consumption of the pulp and extracts from the rind are recommended by some.

Capillary fragility has also been found to vary greatly with the seasons in the newborn, the peak occurring in March and the minimum in August. It has been suggested that this is due to the mothers having received lower amounts of Vitamins K and P during the winter months, when fresh fruits and vegetables are not always easy to obtain. The recommendation has been made that prospective mothers, particularly during the latter months of pregnancy, be sure to consume an adequate amount of the citrus fruits.

In still another study, twenty-two patients were selected who had a variety of respiratory infections, ranging from simple rhinitis to acute follicular tonsillitis and influenza. The researchers made sure that the subjects got *all* the citrus flavonoids now known plus ascorbic acid, since the ascorbic acid alone sometimes does not produce apparent benefits. All but two of the patients made complete recoveries inside of two days, while some recovered in as little as eight hours.

Currently a long-term study is underway regarding the

effects of lemon bioflavonoid complex—also known as lemon peel infusion—on patients with tuberculosis. These patients are also given fresh citrus juices. Results are believed to be highly encouraging.

Even in that most baffling of the respiratory ailments—the common cold—the bioflavonoids appear to be producing spectacular results. In one study, for example, a group of student nurses was given bioflavonoid complex plus Vitamin C while a "control" group received no special additions to their regular diet. The nurses who received the lemon peel extract and Vitamin C had approximately 55 per cent fewer colds than the controls, and when they did get colds the colds lasted for a much shorter time—only 3.9 days on the average as compared with 6.7 days. That's a difference of almost three days per cold, in addition to the fewer colds experienced by the treated group.

Other benefits of the bioflavonoids have been noted in laboratory animals. The addition of crystalline ascorbic acid to the diet of rabbits increased liver glycogen storage 63 per cent as compared with the control group. Lemon juice containing ascorbic acid produced 16 per cent more glycogen than the crystalline ascorbic acid alone. In a variety of tests the bioflavonoids have strengthened heart action and kidney functioning.

Thus it would appear that these amazingly complex substances—some of them vitamins, some chemical combinations that have vitamin characteristics and may aid the development of vitamins within the body—have great powers for the maintenance and restoration of health. They strike right down to the capillaries themselves, tiniest units of the circulatory system which reach directly to every cell.

Most health conscious readers well know the value of the citrus fruits, which contain not only the above-mentioned substances but also other vitamins, amino acids, protopectin, minerals and so on. While confusion regarding their individual natures is still great, some having actually been overlooked or mistaken for others until recently, it appears that all of us will benefit greatly if we consume plenty of their raw juices and consume them as fresh as possible. Valuable elements may be lost within a few hours through oxidation from stored juices, for example, although they are preserved and in some instances actually increased in the raw fruit. Also, it is important to include the pulp when preparing your juices in an electric juicer. This will provide some of the valuable substance in your drink. It would also be good even to gnaw a bit at the rind. And we should do this with both oranges and lemons.

By doing this we will be following Nature's way of preserving the "capillary tree of life"—the nourishment-supplying network upon which real health is based.

Take the common cold, or flu, in another specific example of how juices help. Fruit juices not only satisfy the thirst that has been created by the rise in bodily temperature and the consequent increase of tissue exchange, but they help to neutralize the acid metabolites in the system. This releases into the blood large amounts of mineral salts and vitamins which are essential because of their protective influence on the body.

In people suffering from goiter or other disabilities,

where the rate of metabolism is unusually high, fruit juices serve several purposes. Quite aside from supplying the necessary protective and preventive elements, they have a cooling effect on the body because of the low calorie count and the rapid evaporation of moisture eliminated through the skin. This can also apply to people who suffer greatly from the heat.

In a recent article on the use of raw fruit and vegetable juices, it was stated that "It has been the practice for vegetable juice, as well as fruit juice, to be used extensively on the Continent for therapeutic purposes, and much has been written about its normalizing effect on the intestinal flora and its absorbing effect on the mucous membranes of the intestinal tract. Many systemic conditions in which the breakdown in health appears to be in the direction of the heart and blood vessels, or the kidneys, where there is excessively high blood pressure, or where a rheumatic-arthritic condition interferes with one's activities, respond well to a therapy is which the use of fresh vegetable juice is an important modality of treatment. Where a radical change is required in the internal environment of the body, as, for example, in degenerative nerve diseases where the backlog of faulty nutrition reaches away to heredity, quite substantial quantities of 'protective' food are essential. It will be obvious that whereas two or three glasses of fresh vegetable juice per day might be taken without difficulty, it would entail too great an effort on the part of the digestive and eliminative systems of the body if the equivalent amounts of mineral salts and vitamins had to be obtained through the direct use of the raw vegetables themselves."

Sometimes the question is asked, "Which is the better for me—fruit or vegetable juices?" In general, most people need both, depending upon the condition of their bodies. In the case of elderly people, a word of advice might be well taken here. Fruit juices are sometimes found to be more stimulating than vegetable juices. Therefore, it is wise to use the vegetable juices later in the day. Otherwise, the fruit juices might be found too stimulating just before retiring.

Many people live as though health meant nothing to them. They continue their bad habits until the day of reckoning appears. Then, and only then, do they recognize how precious health is. They are the unfortunate ones for they must work hard to restore what they have deliberately destroyed. Preventative measures are always easier than curative ones.

Some misguided people think they are using preventative measures when they add vitamin tablets to their usual daily diet. There is no doubt that such measures are necessary when the body has been depleted of its reserves, but there is no substitute for the vitamins and minerals which come directly from natural sources. Synthetic vitamins give you only the approximate minimum allowance of one or more specific vitamins. The others, along with the all-important trace elements which are lacking, must be supplied by natural food products.

It is not only the people who are already suffering from disorders of one kind or another who need the benefits of raw juices. There are those others who wake up every morning, tired and dreading to face a new day. Nothing appeals to them—neither work nor play. They resort to stimulants like cigarettes or coffee or alcohol to pull them through the day. They, too, are ill, but they do not recognize it. They need the essential vitamins and minerals fully as much as do the bedridden.

Health—and all that it means in productivity and happiness—is so precious that you should do everything possible in your power to preserve and maintain it. Fortunately, this is enjoyable. The laws of proper nutrition are simple and easy to perform. Each succeeding chapter in this book will give you specific instructions on how best to regain or maintain your health. A careful reading and strict adherence to these principles will pay off many times in health and happiness.

3. The Properties of Raw Juices

*A*S FAR BACK AS 1935, Paul Bragg, who was then a popular health lecturer, said in an article published in Nature's Path, "The continuous and persistent practice of getting the liquid life of fruits and vegetables into the system is one of the secrets of keeping young. They revitalize the blood stream, giving a sparkle to the eye, color to the lips and a spring to the step."

Mary C. Hogle, who has had wide experience treating disease with carrot juice, says, "The most gratifying revelation is that people stricken with serious disorders, cancer included, could by taking enough of it, become strong, active and robust."

Speaking of carrots, Ragnar-Berg, an early diet reform advocate with a learned scientific background, said, "They have some protein, are rich in carbohydrates, potassium, sodium and calcium, there is a high alkali excess, a trace of iodine and a good proportion of all vitamins. They constitute a powerful cleansing food. A large amount of carrot carbohydrate is one of the most effective means of changing the intestinal flora from a putrefactive to a non-putrefactive type."

In the treatment of disease it is evident that acidosis must be corrected as soon as possible and the tissues placed in a position to restore themselves through proper blood alkalinity. Carrot juice has been demonstrated to be best as a rapid alkalinizer and can generally be consumed in large quantities without unpleasant or harmful effects. Carrot juice, because of its minerals and vitamins, is good for conditions where it is a matter of improving the quality of the blood. It is very effective in correcting chronic infections such as tonsilitis, colitis and appendicitis. It is effective in controlling anemia, stones, acidosis, blood poisoning, faulty circulation and ulcers. Rheumatic ailments are a result of nutritional disorders and respond readily to carrot and celery juice treatment. Carrot juice is the richest source of Vitamin A which the body can quickly assimilate, and contains an ample supply of Vitamins B, C, D, E, G and K. It helps to promote the appetite and is an aid to digestion. For the improvement and maintenance of the bony structure of the teeth, it is an invaluable aid. Liberal quantities of carrot juice should be consumed by the nursing mother to enhance the quality of her milk. Because of its strong alkalinity, carrot juice helps to combat fatigue. It is a resistant to infections and a protector of the nervous system. A safe beauty formula and the best rouge is a glass of raw carrot juice, daily.

Celery and its juice presents a prolific source of magnesium, sodium and iron; green celery stalks are more valuable than the branches. Celery is quieting to the nerves and conducive to sound sleep. Raw **parsley** has properties which are essential to oxygen metabolism. Like celery juice, it is a sedative and an effective drug poison eliminator. Parsley is an important cleansing herb, rich in vitamins and strongly alkaline, abounding in iron, calcium, potassium and magnesium. Its value lies chiefly in its stimulating, invigorating life-giving qualities. Because its high concentration may result in a derangement of the nervous system, its juice should be consumed sparingly and always in connection with other raw vegetable juices.

Sulphur and chlorine comprise the most valuable properties of **cabbage;** this combination is effective in cleansing the mucous membrane of the stomach and intestinal tract, but this purifying property is most potent only when cabbage juice is taken in its *raw state*. It is most helpful in obesity. Generous quantities of iron and magnesium abound in **lettuce** juice. Magnesium has exceptional vitalizing powers, particularly in the muscular tissues, the brain and the nerves. Magnesium also assists in the maintenance of the normal fluidity of the blood, in the absence of which proper metabolism is impossible. Fortified also with calcium, potassium, phosphorus, sulphur and silicon, lettuce juice is essential in the proper maintenance of skin, sinews and hair.

In the raw **spinach,** Nature has furnished man with the finest organic material for the cleansing, reconstruction and regeneration of the intestinal tract. Raw spinach juice properly prepared will correct the most aggravated case of constipation within a few days or weeks.

Both vitamins and minerals are necessary to a well balanced diet. As a matter of fact, vitamins control your body's utilization of minerals. In addition, each vitamin seems to have a specific role to play in normal body function. (This will be discussed in greater detail in the following chapter.) On the other hand, if the mineral supply is deficient, there is little benefit from the vitamins. Without vitamins, your body can still appropriate some minerals from the reserve in your system. On the other hand, vitamins are powerless without minerals. Thus, it is essential that one receive the necessary amounts of both.

You should know that your raw fruit and vegetable juices do more than satisfy hunger and please tastes. You should have full understanding that your body is composed of many substances, combined in such manner as to form skin, blood, muscles, bones, hair, gland secretions and all other component parts of the human machine.

You must realize that you are constantly exhausting those substances in many ways—by exertion, by growing, by the normal functions of the organs, elimination and respiration and in other ways. Your task is to restore those lost substances in the proper quantities and form.

If you do your task well, you will see a healthy complexion, strong teeth, a happy smile and unimpaired vigor and vitality. Your well-done dietary work also pays huge dividends in the form of smaller doctor bills, in less frequent colds and minor ailments, in a sunny disposition and in vigorous mental reactions.

How can you, ambitious though you may be, learn the truths necessary for the proper selection of juices?

How can the good be told from the bad?—the worthwhile from the useless? Fundamentally the problem is simple.

Every bit of food taken into the body does either one of three things:

1. It goes into the building of new bone and tissue.

2. It supplies energy and the substances for gland secretions.

3. It merely passes through the digestive and eliminative organs without effect or in a manner which assists or disturbs proper functioning of those organs.

For the average home, where none of the members require any special dietary treatment prescribed by a good physician, the one important rule to remember is:

Serve one juice rich in each of the following classifications at least once every day to every member of the family and, if possible, before every meal.

The foods which supply *energy* are *fats* and *carbohydrates*, the latter term including starch and sugar.

The foods which assist the proper regulation of the *digestive* and *eliminative* organs are *roughage* and *minerals*.

The foods which build *bone and tissue* are *proteins* and those with high mineral content.

One other class of food needed for healthy, happy bodies is *vitamins*.

Due to the fact that ...
our bodies are composed of different amounts
of the different elements
according to our mode of life and our surroundings,
what is a suitable diet for one
is not good for another.

Dr. Fred Humphrey

4. Discover Your Own Deficiencies

*V*ITAMINS ARE a perfect guide to sound nutrition. Balanced intake of vitamins with the wide variety of foods it embraces, assures-balance of all other basic nutrients. When sufficient vitamins are obtained from natural sources, all other elements of good diet are automatically provided. So that you will be able to know your vitamin requirements, I give you the following table:

Recommended Daily Vitamin Requirements

	Vitamin A I.U.	Vitamin B I.U.	Vitamin C I.U.	Vitamin D I.U.	Vit. G Sherman Units
Men	5,000	650	1,500	600	850
Women	5,000	500	1,500	600	850
Pregnant or Nursing Women	7,500	665	2,500	800	1,000
Children*	3,500	350	1,200	700	600

*The term children covers the ages 6 to 12 years. Vitamin requirements of children over 12 are equivalent to those of an adult.

So that you may know which vitamins and minerals are lacking in your diet, I have prepared some tables showing the symptoms which might arise from a deficiency in a particular vitamin. In this way, by comparing the symptoms, you can determine for yourself what your vitamin deficiencies are. Following each is a list indicating the principal plant juice sources of the lacking elements. In a later chapter I shall go into the details of recommended combinations for attacking and arresting the most prevalent chronic ailments. But for now you should study the tables and lists on the following pages for a complete understanding and reflection of just what is wrong with you and how you, yourself, can improve your own health. There is no one as interested in you as you are yourself. That is why I stress this part of the book as being the most important to you for its invaluable self-help qualities.

Vitamin requirements vary somewhat according to size, sex, age and activity. For all practical purposes, however, the above figures representing the average requirements may be safely used. Illness affects vitamin requirements. Consult your physician.

The above daily requirements are recommended for the attainment of the abundant health which is every individual's goal—rather than the mere prevention of deficiency diseases.

Vitamin Deficiency Symptoms and Remedies

VITAMIN A

Vitamin A poor Symptoms	Excellent	Principal Plant Juice Sources of Vitamin A Good	Fair	
Dry, horny skin	Carrots	Artichoke	Okra	Beets	Turnips
Decreased resistance to infection	Escarole	Asparagus	Peppers	Cauliflower	Apples
Formation of gall and kidney stones	Kale	String Beans	Peas	Cucumber	Cranberries
Retarded growth	Parsley	Beet Tops	Romaine	Egg Plant	Grapefruit
Poor tooth formation	Pimento	Broccoli	Pumpkin	Onions	Grapes
Lack of stamina and vigor	Spinach	Cabbage	Tomato	Parsnips	Lemons
Sinus trouble	Sweet Potatoes	Collards	Apricots	Potatoes	Oranges
Catarrh	Turnip Greens	Green Celery & Leaves	Avocado	Radish	Pineapple
Ear abcesses	Watermelon	Chard	Bananas	Rutabaga	Strawberries
Possible sterility in both male and female		Corn, yellow	Cantaloup	Sauerkraut	
Night blindness		Dandelion Greens	Cherries		
Poor appetite		Endive	Plums		
Diarrhea		Lettuce	Peaches		
Digestive disturbances			Raspberries		

Vitamin Deficiency Symptoms and Remedies (cont.)

VITAMIN B

Principal Plant Juice Sources of Vitamin B

Vitamin B poor Symptoms	Excellent	Good		Fair	
General lassitude	Asparagus	String Beans	Rutabaga	Artichoke	Spinach
Constant tiredness	Avocado	Beet greens	Sweet potatoes	Beet roots	Sauerkraut
Loss of vitality		Broccoli	Tomato	Cucumber	Cherries
Slow heart beat		Cabbage	Turnip	Egg plant	Grapes
Poor lactation in nursing		Carrots	Turnip greens	Kale	Orange Peel
mothers		Cauliflower	Watermelon	Kohlrabi	Raisins
Gastric disorders		Celery	Apples	Onions	Raspberries
Diminished peristaltic action		Chard	Bananas	Pumpkin	Strawberries
Nerve degeneration		Dandelion	Cantaloup		
Beri-beri		greens	Grapefruit		
Nervousness		Lettuce	Lemons		
Poor appetite		Okra	Oranges		
		Parsley	Peaches		
		Parsnips	Pears		
		Green peppers	Pineapple		
		Potatoes	Plums		
		Radish	Molasses		
		Romaine			

VITAMIN B₂

	Principal Plant Juice Sources of Vitamin B2		
Vitamin B2 Poor Symptoms	Excellent	Good	Fair
Lack of stamina and vigor	Beet Greens	Broccoli / Turnip Greens	Beets / Corn
Retarded growth	Kale	Cabbage / Watercress	Onions / Pineapple
Insomnia	Spinach	Cucumbers / Apples	Peas / Plums
Indigestion		Carrots / Avocado	Dates / Watermelon
Loss of hair		Celery / Bananas	Grapes / Tangerines
Cataract		Cauliflower / Blueberries	
Poor lactation		Chard / Brussel	
Loss of weight		Dandelion / Sprouts	
Ulceration of tongue		Greens / Cantaloupe	
Pellagra		Escarole / Mustard Greens	
Extreme weakness		Collards / Mint Leaves	
Spinal pain		Lettuce / Lemons	
Ultimate derangement of central		White Potatoes / Orange	
nervous system		Tomato / Pears	
		Turnips	

VITAMIN C

(Vitamin C must be replenished daily. Most ordinary cooking methods entirely destroy it.)
(Vitamin C is also known as Ascorbic Acid. This does not mean that it is obtained from a synthetic source. Vitamin C from any of the plant sources listed in this table could also be designated as Ascorbic Acid)

Vitamin Deficiency Symptoms and Remedies (cont.)

VITAMIN C

Principal Plant Juice Sources of Vitamin C

Vitamin C poor Symptoms	Excellent	Good	Fair
Shortness of breath	Cabbage	Asparagus	Artichoke
Physical weakness	Parsley	String Beans	Beets
Secondary anemia	Green Peas	Carrots	Broccoli
Rapid pulse	Green Peppers	Celery	Brussel Sprouts
Headache	Pimento	Cucumber	Cauliflower
Defective teeth	Rutabaga	Kale	Collards
Tender joints	Tomato	Lettuce	Dandelion Greens
Low resistance to infection	Turnip Greens	Raw Onions	Egg Plant
Lowered hemoglobin	Watercress	Potatoes	Endive
Poor lactation	Cantaloup	Radish	Escarole
Scurvy	Green mint	Spinach	Kohlrabi
Restlessness	Lemons	Sweet Potatoes	Pumpkin
Impaired digestion	Lime	White Turnips	Avocado
	Orange	Apples	Pears
	Raspberries	Apricots	Rhubarb
	Rosehips	Bananas	Papaya
	Strawberries	Cherries	
	Watermelon	Cranberries	
		Black currants	
		Orange Peel	
		Raw Peaches	
		Pineapple	
		Yellow Squash	

VITAMIN D

Vitamin D poor Symptoms	Vitamin D Sources
Poor bone formation Poor tooth formation Constipation Pot belly Bowleggedness Lack of vigor Restlessness Rickets Convulsions Enlarged joints Pigeon breast Curvature of the spine Retarded growth Marked depletion of calcium and phosphorus from the body	Vitamin D is practically non-existant in plants. The best source is sunlight. In the winter it is suggested you add cod liver oil to your juices. Excessive amounts are toxic, so a low potency intake is suggested.

VITAMIN E

Vitamin E poor Symptoms	Vitamin E Plant Juice Sources
Sterility in both sexes Loss of hair Miscarriage Deficient lactation Disturbance during pregnancy Impotence Sexual frigidity Impaired mentality	Spinach Watercress Lettuce Celery Parsley Turnip leaves Wheat Germ Oil

VITAMIN K

Vitamin K poor symptoms	Vitamin K Plant Juice Sources
Retardation of normal coagulation of the blood	Cabbage Kale Cauliflower Spinach

Your body contains an amazing assortment of minerals. Two of them are known to practically everyone—iron and calcium. So often has the need for these minerals been stated that we are apt to think our needs begin and end with them. But they are only two of the more than 20 different minerals that are bound up in the complicated chemistry of our bodies. At least 15 of them perform essential functions. The rest occur in tiny amounts, but scientists feel that these rarer elements may function in ways that are as yet not understood.

It is estimated that our total mineral content weighs about six and one fourth pounds, and that it is worth a mere 97 cents.

The surprising thing about these minerals of ours is that even though there's hardly a handful of them in the body, many of them are basic to the processes that keep us alive. A tiny quantity of calcium, for instance, keeps the heart beating regularly and steadily. Without it the heart beat either becomes erratic or ceases entirely.

Or look at the vital role of iodine. There's scarcely enough of it in the entire system to cover a pin head. But this minute pinch helps to make the difference between a person normal in growth and intelligence and a dwarfed, stupid creature known as a cretin.

It is clear that minerals are just as important in your diet as vitamins. Following is a summary of essential minerals, with iron, calcium, phosphorus and iodine heading the list. These are not only the most important to us of all minerals, but are also the ones which are most likely to be in short supply in our daily diets.

Mineral Deficiency Symptoms and Remedies

IRON

Though iron is stored in the liver, there is a constant demand for it so that a steady supply is needed to keep enough red corpuscles in your body. Therefore careful attention is needed to insure enough iron-rich foods.

Iron-poor Symptoms		Plant Juice Sources
Palpitation of heart upon arising	Dull hearing during menstruation	Wild blackberries
Perspires and flushes on one side	Anemia	Head lettuce
Tendency to colds in head	Asthma	Asparagus
Face alternately flushed and pale	Need for tonics	Currants
Murky yellowish gray face	Neuralgia	Pears
Crying involuntarily	Tense genital organs	Plums
Peevish, whining, disheartened	Face burns, ash gray	Spinach
Exaggerating trivialities	Small of back weak and tender	Sun-dried raisins
Easily fatigued while reading	Suffocation spells	Black Mission Figs
Fearful of losing reason	Soles of feet burn	Strawberries
Alternating pain in kidneys and spleen	Swollen ankles	Cherries
	Fault finding tendency	Okra
	Oppressive respiration	Dandelion leaves
	Bed wetting	Beets
	Partially involuntary discharges	Concord Grapes
	Film before eyes	Kale
	Sore, inflamed eyes	Artichokes
	Desire to carry arms over head	
	Pains in shoulder joints	
	Tired nerves	
	Lively in evening, sluggish mornings	
	Nervous, fussy, hysterical.	
	Partial deafness	
	Desire for long walks in fresh air	
	Food only partially digested	
	Blood in stool	
	Weak rectal muscles	
	Discharges burn	
	Stinging headaches	

Mineral Deficiency Symptoms and Remedies (cont.)

IRON		Plant Juice Sources
Iron-poor Symptoms		
Craving stimulants, indigestibles	Trembling lower limbs	Collards
Fullness, dryness of throat	Cold hands and feet	Leek
Tender nostrils	Intolerable itching	Mustard Greens
Prolapsus of organs	Pulsation in finger tips	Black radishes
Erratic sexual desire	Pulsation in pelvic organs	Brussel Sprouts
Dry hacking cough	Painful breathing	
Tenderness in liver and abdomen	Gas in stomach and bowels	
Lame arms	Tightness in head	
Menstrual pains	Constriction of heart muscles	
	Crave rest, quiet	
	Uterine tumors	
	Weak bladder	
	Sleeplessness at night	
	Sleepy daytimes	
	Hard to please, touchy	
	Heart murmurs	
	Poor equilibrium	
	Pressure in stomach	
	Can see better in the dark	

CALCIUM

Calcium and phosphorus are the body's chief framework materials, used to keep every bone strong and every tooth hard and durable. To some extent we can draw upon the calcium of our bones to tide us over periods when there's a shortage of this mineral. Then calcium is slowly drained from the bones and shunted to other places in the body where it is needed. There is an obvious danger in tapping this store too frequently, for we will weaken our skeletal framework.

Throughout life calcium is a "must." There are three times, however, when the need for it is of prime importance—during pregnancy, breast feeding and the years of growth.

Adults also need adequate supplies of calcium every day because there is a constant drain of it from the body. Only through proper diet can enough of this mineral be taken in to equalize the quantity lost.

Do we get enough calcium to meet our needs? Most authorities agree that there is a widespread lack of calcium in the average diet, and that most of us need to boost our calcium intake.

Calcium-poor Symptoms		Plant Juice Sources
Laborious thinking	Slow blood clotting	Turnip leaves
Listlessness	Incoherent speech	Cabbage
Ennui	Earthy complexion	Green peppers
Looking into distance	Stinging pains in genitals	Lemons
Sighing	Sluggish blood circulation	Limes
Brooding	Sensitive to moisture	Onions
Fear	Afternoon headache	Oranges
Getting into a rut	Dizzy in open air	Rhubarb
Lacking executive power	Staggering upon arising	Spinach
Complaining	Early sleepiness	Cranberries
Distrust	Palpitation upon ascending stairs	Gooseberries
Pessimism	Varicose veins	Grapes
Weak will power	Icy sensation in spine	Lettuce
Grief over trivialities	Sour body odors	Plums
Lack of courage		Asparagus

Mineral Deficiency Symptoms and Remedies (cont.)

CALCIUM

Calcium-poor Symptoms		Plant Juice Sources
Mental aggravation	Slowness in walk	Cucumbers
Hemorrhages	Slimy salivation	Peaches
Trembling	Sores do not heal	Radishes
Soft bones	Lame ligaments	Celery
Deformities	Slow convalescence	Swiss Chard
Chilblains	Catarrh	Carrots
Ugly scars	Discharges	Sauerkraut
One limb shorter than other	Pus formation	Lima beans
Cysts	Suppuration	Cauliflower
		Currants
		Kale
		Kohlrabi

PHOSPHORUS

Scarcely any of our vital processes take place without phosphorus. It occurs in the protoplasm and nucleus of every cell. It also enters into the formation of the body's complex protein and fat compounds, as well as the plasma and other body fluids. About two pounds of this mineral are needed to fill the body's requirements.

Phosphorus-poor Symptoms	Plant Juice Sources
Neuralgia	Red cabbage
Impotence	Corn
Pale face	Peas
Dislike for work	Savoy cabbage
Feeling there is something wrong	Concord
Hardening of wax in ears	grapes
Numbness in some part of body	Carrots
Dreading the future	Squash
Prostration during period	Raisins
Insensibility to pain	Mustard
Dislike for opposite sex	Greens
Unresponsiveness to sexual stimulation	Mushrooms
	Pumpkin
	Okra
	Watercress
	Parsley
	Cucumbers

Phosphorus-poor Symptoms	Plant Juice Sources
Bronchitis	
Jaundice	
Emaciated arms and legs	
Variable body temperature	
Slowness in learning to walk	
Weakness, parchment-like appearance in young girls	
Neurasthenia	
Paralysis	
Beanlike knots form in glands in neck	
Loss of control of hand or arm.	

IODINE

No mineral shortage shows up quite so spectacularly as does that of iodine. Practically every molecule of it is greedily snatched from the blood stream by the thyroid gland to use in the powerful thyroid hormone known as thyroxin. Either too much or too little can cause difficulties to the body.

Mineral Deficiency Symptoms and Remedies (cont.)

IODINE

Iodine-poor Symptoms		Plant Juice Sources	
Swelling in throat, goiter	Dullness under shoulder blade	Artichokes	Broccoli
Pale doughy, dry, hot scaly skin	Numbness in fingers or hands	Carrots	Chard
Mind slow, salivation frothy	Swelling of feet or toes	Garlic	Celery
Arms numb, scars break open	Preference to standing	Green grapes	Lettuce
Heart, chest and head pressure	Great occasional prostration	Sea lettuce	Kale
Urine turbid, violet-yellowish-green	Enlarged glands	Dulse	Red Cabbage
	Stinging migratory pain sensations	Mushrooms	Savoy Cabbage
Throbbing in arteries	Pulse slow, rapid alternately	Bartlett Pears	Strawberries
Neuralgic pains in heart	Excessive hunger	Pineapple	Tomatoes
Neuralgic pains in uterus lining	Squinting of eyes	Avocado	Watercress
Sweet and putrid saliva, alternately	Tenderness of lower ribs	Potato skin	Asparagus
Ailments usually on left side	Greasy taste in mouth	Chives	Brussel Sprouts
Hurried, short respiration	Dislike for moisture	White onions	Chervil
Tearing, jumping or wavy pain sensation in nerves	Watery discharge from nose		

SODIUM

Sodium-poor Symptoms		Plant Juice Sources
Physical exhaustion	Hay Fever	Carrots
Cold drinks produce pain	Throat ailments	Celery
Stiff and short ligaments	Bloating	Okra
Gout		
Indigestion		
Vomiting		

48

			Spinach
Rheumatism	White spots palms of hands	Poor smell	Strawberries
Frontal Headache	Catarrh of throat	Catarrh of nose	Apples
Dry Tongue	Flying in rage over trivialities	Fear of drafts	Asparagus
Dry Skin	Poor digestion of fat, starches and sweets	Murky complexion	Beets
Cold Feet	Sulphur foods produce gas	Burning face	Cucumbers
Sleepy during Day	Breath has sewer odor	Sciatica	Gooseberries
Heart bothers	Tendency to skin eruptions	Jerking of eyelids	Plums
Gas in the stomach	Catarrh of lungs	Requires newer and newer glasses	Radishes
Drum stomach	Irritated nerves	Numbness	Swiss Chard
Irritability	Fear	Cramps	Turnips
Fearing downward motion	Chlorosis	Stomach Ulcers	
Acid stomach	Excessive thirst	Hardening of Arteries	
Cannot read small print	Constipation	Neuritis	
Confusion of mind	Bursting headaches	Dry salivary glands	
Weariness, tired spells	Falling hair	Color changes of urine	
Hysterical moods	Asthma	Low specific gravity of urine	
Dizziness			
Mental depression			
Melancholia, "Blues"			

POTASSIUM

Potassium nourishes the muscular system, and (united with phosphorus) the brain cells. It is a healer of injuries, alkalizes the system, and helps heart functions.

Potassium-poor Symptoms		Plant Juice Sources	
Weak heart	Distress in pit of stomach	Bitter taste in mouth	Chervil	Asparagus
Periodic headache	Sunken, red, lusterless eyes	Nausea from excitement	Chicory	Broccoli
Flying pains			Watercress	Kale

Mineral Deficiency Symptoms and Remedies (cont.)

POTASSIUM

Potassium-poor Symptoms		Plant Juice Sources
Dropsical ankles	Feeling of sand in eyes	Dandelion leaves
Dry parched throat	Stinging pains in left ear	Beet tops
Profuse perspiration	Greenish ropy sputum	Blueberries
Atrophied muscles	Pain in lower back	Cabbage
Inward fever	head	Cocoanut
Crawling in feet	Crawling under roots	Endive
Itchy dry skin, scabs	of teeth	Lettuce
Excema on legs	Restlessness at night	Mint leaves
Painful postules	Great rush to take	Parsley
Angry ulcers	off shoes	Spinach
Sensitive corns	Cramp pains in heart	Pineapple
Pain in side	Organs feel as	Swiss Chard
Throbbing feet	though hanging	Carrots
Nosebleed	Constriction in urethra	Artichokes
Jerking in limbs	Tingling in rectum	Brussel Sprouts
Gnawing sensations	Distention of stomach	Grapes
Pyorrhea	Desire for cold water	Green peppers
Frothy saliva	Desire for sour food	Leek
Tendency to blister	One ear red, other pale	Rhubarb
Itching around scars	Throbbing over eyes	Celery
Defective bowel movements	Crawling under skin	Turnip leaves
Cannot digest sugar well	Tickling in nose	Wild black cherries
	Enlarged ovaries	Yellow tomatoes
	Swollen testicles	
	Diabetes	
	Sleeplessness	
	Liver trouble	
	Kidney trouble	
	Gall stones	
	Female weakness	
	Neurasthenia	
	Dropsy	
	Displacement of womb	
	Weak uterine muscles	
	Weak and sagging ligaments	
	Pain runs from head to fingertips	
	Cramps	
	Organic heart disease	
	Loose hanging stomach	
	Shrinking of heart valves	

MAGNESIUM

Magnesium-poor Symptoms		Plant Juice Sources
Inflated intestines	Oily perspiration	Oranges
Catarrhal discharges	Going to sleep over work	Lemons
Sour odor of bowel contents	Intolerance to dress pressure	Grapefruit
Muddy, sickly complexion	Burning sensation in mouth	Tangerines
Emaciated look	Restless eyes and fingers	Limes
Acid blood, body gas	Tendency to motion sickness	Plums
Constipation	Chilly after retiring	Spinach
Gas-disturbed sleep	Falling sensations	Dandelion
Nervous ailments	Creepy feeling, standing, sitting	leaves
Fainting spells	Strong desire for tart drinks	Mustard
Peritonitis	Desire for ducking head in water	greens
Cholera	Diarrhea	Lettuce
Passion, fear, grief	Neuralgia	Apples
Alternating toothache	Frequent burning urination	Grapes
Earthy taste in mouth	Pale Urine	Savoy
Aching neck and shoulder muscles	Weak thumbs	cabbage
Yellow expectorations	Sleep with eyes half open	Pomegranate
Late scanty period flow	Jerky muscle twitches	Sugar beet
Yellowish whites of eyes	Jaundice	tops
Hardening of the liver	Over-heated blood	Cherries
Weakness of abdominal muscles	Allergic to woolen garments	Corn
Swimming sensation in head	Jerky neck and jaw muscles	Peaches
		Pears

51

Mineral Deficiency Symptoms and Remedies (cont.)

SILICON

Silicon-poor symptoms		Plant Juice Sources
Tumors	Rheumatism	Calimyrna
Tuberculosis	Running sores	figs
Hay fever	Excessive perspiration	Lettuce
Coughing, wakefulness at	Soles of feet itch	Strawberries
night	Headaches	Mustard
Boils	Painful piles	greens
Neurasthenia	Parched lips	White
Lame sensation in small of	Brittle, dull hair	onions
back	Polyps	Parsnips
Frequent urination	Ovary troubles	Olives
Weak lower limbs	Enlarged liver	Asparagus
Painful scant menstruation	Dizziness	Dandelion
Fingertips burn	Cold on left side of body	greens
Pain in genitals	Staggering at right side in	Cabbage
Drug addiction	walking	Cucumbers
Nervous exhaustion	Small, rapid pulse	Radishes
Impotence	Prostatic pains	Alfalfa
	Premature emissions	
	Loose gums	
	Yellow skin on face	
	Flying pains in chest and	
	abdomen	
	Twitching of left eyelid	
	Fainting spells	
	Sore thighs	
	Sleepiness during afternoon	
	Throbbing sensation in head	
	and chest	
	Large warts	
	Teeth sensitive to cold	
	Itchy ears	
	No ambition for brain work	
	Lumpy sores	
	Cracked finger nails	

CHLORINE

Chlorine-poor Symptoms	Plant Juice Sources
Slow digestion of fats and sweets	Asparagus
Bloody saliva and urine	Carrots
Always hungry	Celery
Hot flashes	Red and white cabbage
Deafness, roaring in ears	Cucumbers
Pyorrhea	Lettuce
Nervous prostration	Radishes
Heavy limbs	Spinach
Bladder troubles	Collards
Distress in heart	Ripe olives
Bloating in abdomen	Tomatoes
Mucus forms in throat	Sauerkraut
Frontal headaches, travel backward	Kale
Purple extremities	
Blue lips	
Grayish nail roots	
Tension in stomach	
Upper lip quivers	
Facial muscles twitch	
Bones ache	
Constipation	
Sore, burning mouth	
Worries, mutters, moans in sleep	
Likes acid foods and drink	
Rheumatic pains in muscles	
Burning in kidneys	

Mineral Deficiency Symptoms and Remedies (cont.)

FLUORINE

Fluorine-poor Symptoms		Plant Juice Sources
Decay of bones and teeth	Dirty, oily, yellowish skin pigment	Cabbage
Tumors in liver, spleen	Puffed, swollen body parts	Cauliflower
Stones in kidneys	Puffed neck, head, skin, lower abdomen	Garlic
Tumors in internal organs	Loose, tender spongy gums	Sauerkraut
Hard crusts form in nose	Piggish odor or smell in nose	Spinach
Urethral catarrh	Great aversion to darkness	Sprouts
Bony growths in ears	Bilious after drinking cold water	Watercress
Hard shrunken prostate	Ailments with nails, bunions, eyelashes	Endive
Sclerosis	Brown yellow spots on skin	Chervil
Sterility	Pain in the ball of the eyes	Blackeyed beans
Enlarged uterus	Sticking eyelids	Avocado
Deformities of spine	Puffy lips, neck and eyes	Juniper berries
Pus formation	Decay taste sensation in mouth	Quince
Dilated blood vessels	Bleeding gums	Sea cabbage
Mucus and ammonia in urine	Trouble in hearing	
Puffy obesity	Troubled eyesight	
Ulcerative processes	Red, swollen nose	
Rheumatism in bones, numbness	Numbness of hands, protruding eyeballs	
Gluey, swollen eyelids	Clammy, decayed sweat	
	Darker blood than usual	
	Dark tongue	
	Milk makes sick and bilious	
	Cramp legs, tottering	
	Poor eyesight	
	Hypertrophy of the spleen	
	Tendency to diphtheria	
	Bone tumors	
	Tumors in cerebellar structures	
	Paralysis	
	Ulceration	
	Degenerative processes	
	Backwardness in manners	
	Glandular catarrh	

SULPHUR

Sulphur-poor Symptoms	Plant Juice Sources
Gloomy in morning	Red cabbage
Granulated eyelids	Carrots
Full of tough mucus	Chestnuts
Continual trouble with throat	Cocoanut
Continual trouble with stomach	Figs
Continual trouble with colon	Nuts
Acid stomach	Oranges
Gas generation	Spinach
Fitful indigestion	Brussel
Craving cold water over feet	sprouts
Strong light irritates	Chervil
Red, shiny nosetip	Cranberries
Pulsations in liver, spleen, uterus	Dill
Swelling in abdomen	Endive
Saliva fetid, throat burning	Mustard
Rosy appearance, yet full of pain	greens
Urine fetid and green	Leeks
Milk causes nausea	Marjoram
Feet burn, nerves irritated	Nasturtium
Tingling, chiming in ears	Red
Heart palpitates upon climbing	raspberries
Dropsical, with cold in knees	Loganberries
Night sweats on chest	Sorrel
Moisture soothes, rush confuses	Rhubarb
Severe motion produces stiff neck	Turnips
Burning sensation in abdomen	Turnip
Sleepy, dull, torpid in morning	greens
Dryness of skin, gums	Watercress
Swelling of liver, spleen, uterus	Cauliflower
	Onions
	Parsnips
	Peaches
	Radishes
	Rutabagas
	Apples
	Asparagus
	Cherries
	Cucumbers
	Gooseberries
	Grapes
	Horseradish
	Potatoes
	Roebuck
	berries
	Blackberries
	Dewberries

Mineral Deficiency Symptoms and Remedies (cont.)

MANGANESE

Manganese-poor Symptoms		Plant Juice Sources
Gout at night, throatal pain	Abdomen full of wind	Chives
Dry catarrh, falling symptoms	Greasy taste in mouth	Watercress
Gripping drawing pain sensations	Spasmodic nerves	Endive
Drowsiness	Disturbed equilibrium	Nasturtium
Itching in hollow of knees	Hot face	Almonds
Swellings have glossy appearance	Red and swollen eyes	Chestnuts
Burning in body, profuse sweat	Shrunken brain	Walnuts
Nerve pain from shoulder to toes	Weak cerebellum	Parsley
Great tenderness of nipples	Erratic taste functions	Peppermint leaves
Heart palpitation	Disagreeable	Wintergreen
Excreta yellowish, drawing in anus	Tasting milk produces distension of stomach	Acorns
Claylike sediment in urine	Difficult breathing	Blackeyed beans
Stomach contracts, cannot hold food	Fainting spells	Butternuts
Enlargement of ovaries, fallen womb	Glands swell	French beans
Lower limbs lifeless at times	Bones crack	
Lameness, stiffness in arms	Eyes drowsy	
Motion produces rushing sound	Weakness in rectum muscles	
Cold food produces pressure in stomach	Itching is worse during and after perspiration	
Boiling, bubbling sensation		

The following table, unlike others of its kind, is figured in ordinary kitchen weights and measures and requires no further interpretation. It will be found useful as a basis for judging *relative* vitamin values of raw juices and as a guide in marketing and menu-planning. It will also serve as a key for computing the vitamin value of various juice combinations found in this book.

Variety, soil, climate, maturity, preservation and storage of foods all affect vitamin content, hence the juices do not have a fixed vitamin value, but rather a range of values. For practical purposes, however, it is customary to put single vitamin values on common foods. The single values in the table which follows, result from a correlation of the most recent and reliable summaries, and are, in the opinion of the author, the most representative figures obtainable.

Table of Estimated Vitamin Content of Common Foods

FOOD	QUANTITY	International Units A	B1	C	D	S.U.* G
Alfalfa	1 cup, 4 oz.	18,000	—	—	—	500
Apples, raw	1 med.	75	23	200	—	20
Apricots, fresh	1 med.	1,840	4	25	—	16
Artichokes, French	1 med.	250	70	300	—	8
Artichokes, Jerusalem	1 med.	—	46	200	—	—
Asparagus, blanched (white)	1 cup	68	83	1,508	—	—

*Sherman Units

Note: Where dashes occur in the foregoing table (—), the vitamin content is either *insignificant, completely lacking* or *cannot be indicated in any reliable value at this writing*.

Values are for raw foods.

Values should be taken as applying to foods that are reasonably fresh. Allowance should be made for fruits and vegetables which are known to have been stored for a considerable period.

| FOOD | QUANTITY | International Units | | | | S.U.* |
		A	B1	C	D	G
Asparagus, green	1 cup	960	116	1,600	—	80
Avocado	1 med.	200	70	400	—	110
Banana, raw	1 med.	375	25	200	—	40
Beans, lima, fresh	1 cup	1,150	264	1,380	—	230
Beans, string, (snap) fresh	1 cup	2,300	57	690	—	92
Beans, wax, butter, or yellow	1 cup	820	60	320	—	75
Bean sprouts	1 cup	10	20	975	—	92
Beets, diced	1 cup	140	48	400	—	25
Beet tops (same as Chard)						
Blackberries, fresh	1 cup	230	10	300	—	—
Blueberries	1 cup	150	21	160	—	7
Broccoli	1 cup	8,000	45	1,600	—	150
Brussel sprouts	1 cup	1,100	50	1,800	—	—
Cabbage, raw, white	1 cup	—	50	2,000	—	15
Cabbage, raw, green	1 cup	100	50	3,000	—	30
Cantaloup (See Melon, musk)						
Carrots, fresh, raw diced	1 cup	2,700	32	160	—	32
Cauliflower	¼ hd. 3 oz.	25	50	1,500	—	35
Cauliflower	1 cup	50	100	3,000	—	70
Celery, fresh, blanched, (diced)	1 cup	20	20	200	—	—
Celery, fresh, green	1-7" stalk	500	5	50	—	5
Celery, fresh, green (diced)	1 cup	2,000	20	200	—	20
Chard	1 cup	20,000	30	1,120	—	75
Cherries, fresh, Bing	1 cup	160	20	460	—	—
Cherries, fresh, Royal Anne	1 cup	390	30	690	—	—
Chicory (same content as Endive)						
Chives	1 tspn.	—	—	40	—	—
Cocoanut, shredded, fresh	1 cup	—	16	160	—	80
Cocoanut, milk, fresh	1 cup	—	—	140	—	—

| FOOD | QUANTITY | International Units | | | | S.U.* |
		A	B1	C	D	G
Collards	1 cup	10,000	100	10,000	—	200
Corn, sweet, white (Gentleman)	1 cup	100	90	400	—	—
Corn, yellow	1 cup	1,000	70	400	—	35
Cranberries, fresh	1 cup	70	—	400	—	—
Cucumbers, fresh	1 large	20	110	720	—	2
Currants, black, fresh	1 cup	—	11	4,400	—	—
Currants, red, fresh	1 cup	—	16	1,100	—	—
Dandelion greens	1 cup	18,000	36	1,400	—	150
Dates, fresh	1 cup	153	51	—	—	51
Eggplant, diced	1 cup	92	56	464	—	44
Endive	1 stalk, 6"	1,900	23	135	—	45
Escarole (same content as Endive)						
Fennel	1 cup	—	—	1,062	—	—
Figs, fresh, chopped	1 cup	150	50	75	—	100
Garlic	1 clove	—	—	20	—	—
Gooseberries, fresh, green	1 cup	760	56	680	—	—
Grapefruit, juice, fresh	1 cup	—	45	2,000	—	20
Grape juice	1 cup	—	15	60	—	60
Guava, fresh, stoned	1 med.	200	14	1,500	—	2
Horse radish,	1 tblsp.	—	—	350	—	—
Huckleberries	1 cup	—	—	1,600	—	—
Kale	1 cup	10,000	24	1,440	—	400
Kohlrabi	1 cup	—	16	1,200	—	—
Kumquats	1 med.	—	—	135	—	—
Leek	1 cup	119	56	980	—	—
Lemons	1 med.	—	20	1,100	—	—
Lemons, rind, grated	1 tblsp.	—	3	375	—	—
Lettuce, Romaine	1 av. head	13,000	40	200	—	100
Lettuce, Iceberg, whole head	Entire	600	80	360	—	68
Limes	1 med.	100	—	400	—	—
Loganberries	1 cup	—	—	1,600	—	—
Mangoes	1 med.	1,500	30	600	—	20
Melon, Musk, Rocky Ford	½ med.	770	73	1,200	—	80

FOOD	QUANTITY	International Units A	B1	C	D	S.U.* G
Melon, Honeydew	½ med.	—	—	1,420	—	—
Mushrooms, fresh	1 cup	—	100	—	—	—
Mustard greens	1 lb.	92,000	207	6,500	—	675
Nectarines, yellow, fresh	1 lb.	4,800	—	480	—	—
Okra	1 lb.	1,840	184	1,380	—	800
Olives, green, chopped	1 cup	892	10	—	—	—
Olives, ripe, Mission	1 cup	782	10	—	—	—
Onions, spring	1 med.	500	—	75	—	—
Onions, mature, chopped	1 cup	—	24	300	—	60
Oranges, fresh, juice	1 cup	625	62	825	—	15
Oranges, rind, grated	1 tblsp.	87	18	225	—	3
Papaya	8 oz.	5,750	58	1,970	—	1,380
Parsley, chopped	1 tblsp.	1,000	—	222	—	—
Parsnips	1 cup	—	100	1,035	—	—
Peaches, fresh, white	1 med.	—	5	160	—	—
Peaches, fresh, yellow	1 med.	900	28	70	—	—
Pears, fresh, raw	1 cup	2,000	275	900	—	172
Peppers, green	1 med.	1,500	69	2,000	—	40
Peppers, red	1 med.	7,000	10	2,700	—	14
Persimmon	1 med.	2,550	—	400	—	—
Pimentos	1 cup	28,000	40	10,800	—	56
Pineapple juice	1 cup	200	70	700	—	20
Plantains	1 med.	500	25	200	—	40
Plums, fresh	1 med.	180	12	50	—	5
Pomegranate	1 med.	—	—	450	—	—
Potatoes, old, white	1 med.	80	50	400	—	40
Potatoes, new, white	1 med.	80	75	500	—	40
Potatoes, yellow (sweet)	1 med.	7,000	60	800	—	60
Prunes, uncooked, raw	1 med.	98	—	20	—	—
Pumpkin	1 cup	380	30	120	—	12
Quinces	1 med.	—	—	220	—	—
Radishes	1 cup	—	40	800	—	20
Raisins	1 cup	112	84	—	—	52
Raspberries, fresh	1 cup	2 0	18	660	—	—

| FOOD | QUANTITY | International Units | | | | S.U.* |
		A	B1	C	D	G
Rhubarb, fresh	1 cup	230	18	360	—	—
Rutabagas, white	1 cup	—	35	900	—	—
Rutabagas, yellow	1 cup	60	35	900	—	—
Salsify	1 cup	—	—	350	—	—
Sauerkraut, juice, fresh	1 cup	—	—	640	—	—
Scallions (see Onions, spring)						
Spinach, fresh, raw	1 lb.	90,000	207	5,850	—	598
Squash, summer (white)	1 cup	690	32	138	—	62
Squash, winter, (Hubbard, yellow)	1 cup	7,000	32	138	—	62
Srawberries, fresh	1 cup	—	—	2,900	—	—
Tangerines	1 med.	280	22	560	—	7
Tomato juice	1 cup	7,064	60	650	—	10
Turnip, white	1 cup	—	24	1,200	—	24
Turnip, yellow	1 cup	40	24	1,200	—	24
Turnip greens	1 lb.	46,000	180	13,800	—	550
Watercress	1 bunch	4,000	56	880	—	—
Watermelon	1 slice (¾" x 6")	—	40	300	—	25

There are incurable patients
but no incurable diseases,
for when their causes are removed
the symptoms will disappear like shadows before sunshine
and there will be nothing left to cure.

Dr. J. T. Work

5. Recipes for Health

$\mathcal{I}$T IS IMPORTANT to realize the specific value of various juice combinations and their role in the maintenance of health. Now that I have discussed the function of each of the minerals and vitamins separately, I will analyse their effect when combined in juices.

We must make note here that you can drink as much juice as you wish. You cannot have too much, only too little.

RAW CARROT JUICE is a rich source of Vitamin A. It normalizes the entire system and is a natural solvent for ulcerous conditions. When combined with beet, lettuce and turnip, it is a powerful blood builder. Depending upon the condition of the individual, raw carrot juice may be taken indefinitely and in quantities of from one to six pints a day. As has been pointed out previously, besides being the richest source of Vitamin A, it also contains an ample supply of Vitamins B, C, D, E, G, and K. It helps to promote the appetite and is an aid to digestion.

Carrot juice is also a valuable aid in the improvement and maintenance of the bone structure of the teeth. It is especially good for nursing mothers as it enriches the quality of the milk.

RAW POTASSIUM BROTH includes the vegetables richest in potassium: carrots, celery, parsley and spinach.

The organic minerals and salts in the above mentioned combination of potassium broth, embrace practically the entire range of those required by the body. It is excellent for reducing excessive acidity in the stomach. It is probably the most complete food for nearly every condition of the human organism.

It is both palatable and nourishing for people too ill to assimilate other food.

Potassium broth is particularly beneficial to women. Women of all ages should drink at least one pint daily. This element seems to have particular affinity to the blood stream and is much help to women who suffer from premenstrual headaches. These headaches are usually due to disturbed condition of the blood stream due to the presence of excessive starches and sugars in the diet. If these can be eliminated preceding and during these periods and an abundance of juices, particularly raw potassium, taken daily, it will prove very beneficial. Potassium broth is helpful during the menopause periods also.

The addition of a little pure cream will make the juice tastier for those who do not like it plain.

The formula for this is:

7 ounces carrot juice		2 ounces parsley
4 " celery		3 " spinach

APPLE JUICE tones and cleanses the body. It is high in

potassium, sodium and phosphorus. It metabolizes fatty foods to aid digestion, is fine for the kidneys and promotes intestinal activity. It is an excellent blood purifier, good in cases of constipation, sluggish liver, skin eruptions, poor complexion and anemia.

CELERY JUICE is a natural nerve tonic. It is high in potassium, calcium, sodium and phosphorus. It provides food for blood cells and is a builder and blood cleanser. It keeps calcium in distribution, which is an aid in arthritic conditions.

CARROT AND CELERY JUICE combined cleanse the system of excessive acid or acidosis which would lead to degenerative troubles.

The chemical content of this combination is particularly efficient in the regeneration of the tissues, especially those connected with the ligaments of the joints and the nervous system generally.

Celery contains more than four times as much organic sodium as it does calcium, which is why it is so valuable in the treatment of arthritis. Arthritis is the accumulation of inorganic calcium in the cartilage of the joints as a result of years of eating devitalized foods, such as flour, starches and refined sugars. Sufficient organic sodium will tend to prevent this.

Celery and its combinations are a great aid to arthritics provided that during the course of the treatment, which may extend from a few weeks to several months, every kind and variety of flour, starch and sugar is eliminated from the diet.

In the case of nervous afflictions resulting from the degeneration of the sheathing of the nerves, the abundant use of carrot and celery juice will help to restore these to their normal states and thus alleviate or remove the affliction.

If there is an inadequate supply of sulphur, iron and calcium in the diet, or if there is a supply of these but in devitalized inorganic form, then asthma, rheumatism, hemorrhoids and other disturbances will result. Unbalanced proportions of sulphur and phosphorus in the diet will create conditions of mental irritability, neurasthenia and even insanity.

CARROT, CELERY AND PARSLEY JUICE has the same effect as carrot and celery, but parsley is a more intensive cleanser of the kidneys. It is a specific food for the adrenal glands and has a very powerful therapeutic effect on the optic nerves, on the brain nerves and on the entire sympathetic nerve system.

Concentrated parsley juice should never be taken alone in greater quantities than one tablespoon at a time. It is exceedingly potent and if taken in excess, will overstimulate the nervous system. It should be taken in reasonable quantities with carrot and celery juice. It then intensifies the food value of this combination and will assist as a corrective in the adjustment of eye trouble. It will also cleanse the kidneys and stimulate them to normal function.

CARROT AND BEET JUICE: The quantity of iron in red beets is not high but is of a quality that furnishes excellent food for the red corpuscles of the blood. The sodium content is high while the calcium content is low, which is a valuable proportion for maintaining the solubility of calcium. This is especially important in the case of varicose veins and hardening of the arteries where inorganic calcium has been permitted to accumulate in the system and has formed deposits within the blood vessels. It is also helpful in cases of high blood pressure and other forms of heart trouble in which the blood vessels have thickened.

The combination of carrot and beet juice furnishes a good percentage of phosphorus and sulphur, plus potassium and other alkaline elements. This together with the high content of Vitamin A, completes what is probably the best natural builder of the blood cells, particularly the red blood corpuscles.

The addition of some pure cocoanut milk extracted from the meat of the cocoanut added to the carrot and beet juice, makes a combination that is not only an intensive body builder, but has even more potent qualities as a cleanser of the kidneys and gall bladder. If properly prepared, this combination contains the alkaline elements potassium, sodium, calcium, magnesium and iron in abundance, and the other elements phosphorus, sulphur, silicon and chlorine, in ample and correct proportions.

When we add cucumber juice to carrot and beet juice, we have one of the finest cleansing and healing materials for the gall bladder, the liver, kidneys, the prostrate and other sex glands. Again, all flour and sugar must be eliminated from the diet if the full value of these juice combinations is to be derived, particularly in the case of gall stones and kidney stones. One or two pints of this combination of carrot, beet and cucumber juice daily, will dissolve these stones in the course of a few weeks or months and thereby eliminate the need of surgery for their removal.

During the period of treatment it is advisable to eliminate meat also from the diet.

CARROT AND CABBAGE JUICE: Cabbage contains a

high content of sulphur and chlorine and a rather large percentage of iodine. Sulphur and chlorine combined cleanse the mucous membrane of the stomach and intestinal tract. Cabbage juice should be taken in its raw state and without the addition of salt.

In the event that there is gas or other distress after drinking raw cabbage juice either straight or in combination with other raw vegetable juices, it is an indication that an abnormal condition exists in the intestinal tract. Then it is advisable to cleanse the intestines thoroughly by drinking carrot or carrot and spinach juice daily for two or three weeks and use the enema. Once the intestines are able to assimilate this juice, it will be an invaluable cleanser and of great help to those who are overweight.

Raw cabbage juice added to carrot juice forms an excellent source of Vitamin C as a cleansing medium, particularly where infection of the gums with resultant pyorrhea is present.

We know that boiling or dehydrating juices destroys the effectiveness of the vitamins, minerals and salts. One-half pint of raw cabbage juice, properly prepared, contains more organic food value than does two hundred pounds of cooked or canned cabbage.

CARROT AND RADISH JUICE AND HORSERADISH SAUCE is a cleanser of abnormal mucus in the system. This is the best known method by which mucus can be effectively dissolved without damage to the membranes. One-half teaspoonful of fresh horseradish should be taken twice a day between meals. The horseradish sauce should be prepared fresh and should not be used when it is more than one week old. It must be kept cold and moistened with plenty of lemon juice. *Never add vinegar.* Commercial vinegar destroys the tissues of the membranes lining the stomach and intestines.

Do not mix anything else besides lemon juice to the horseradish; nothing to dilute it, nor should anything else be taken to drink for a few moments after eating it. One-half teaspoonful should be taken during the morning and one-half teaspoonful during the afternoon daily. This will at first cause a sensation in the head which will create copious tears, depending upon the volume of mucus in the sinus cavities and other parts of the system.

This should be continued for weeks or months, until the horseradish sauce can be eaten without any sensation resulting from it. When there is no sensation, then we know that it has practically completed the dissolution of the mucus. This is a very effective natural means to cure the cause of sinus mucus.

The juice of fresh radishes including the tops, is too potent to be taken alone. It should be mixed with carrot juice, in connection with which it will have the effect of soothing and healing the membranes and cleansing the body of the mucus which the horseradish sauce has dissolved. At the same time it will help regenerate and restore the mucus membranes to their normal state.

Radishes contain nearly one-third potassium, more than one-third sodium and iron and magnesium, which heal and soothe the mucous membranes.

Surgery removes the mucus in sinus troubles, but it does not remove the cause. On the other hand, the horseradish sauce will dissolve the cause. Mucus is the result of drinking too much milk and eating concentrated starches, bread and cereals in excess.

LETTUCE JUICE has great quantities of iron and magnesium. Iron is the most active element in the body and it must be renewed more frequently than any other. Iron is stored in the liver and spleen where it is ready for any sudden demand of the body, such as the rapid formation of red blood corpuscles where there is a heavy loss of blood. The iron is also stored in the liver for the purpose of furnishing mineral compounds to any part of the body from which they may suddenly and rapidly diminish as after a hemorrhage.

The storage of iron in the spleen, however, acts as an electric storage battery where the blood is recharged with the necessary electricity for its proper functions.

The high content of magnesium in lettuce has exceptional vitalizing powers, particularly in the muscular tissues, the brain and the nerves. Organic salts of magnesium are cell builders, especially of the nerve system and of the tissues of the lungs. They also assist in maintaining the normal fluidity of the blood and other functions without which it would be impossible for metabolism to operate properly.

When combined with carrot juice, the properties of lettuce juice are intensified by the addition of Vitamin A and sodium. Sodium assists in maintaining the calcium in the lettuce in constant solution until utilized by the body.

Lettuce contains more than 38% potassium, nearly 15% calcium, more than 5% iron, about 6% magnesium, more than 9% phosphorus, an ample supply of sulphur, more than 8% silicon.

Drinking daily an abundance of carrot, lettuce and spinach juice combined, will furnish food to the nerves and roots of the hair; which is the only means by which the growth of the hair can be stimulated. The combination of carrot, lettuce and alfalfa juice is another efficient juice therapy for the growth of hair and restoration of its natural color.

SPINACH JUICE is a most vital food for the entire digestive tract: the stomach, duodenum and small intestines and the large intestine or colon.

The use of manufactured chemical purgatives for the cleansing of the intestinal tract acts as an irritant, stimulating the muscles of the intestines to expell the irritant and removing other matter lodged therein. Eventually stronger and stronger laxatives are needed. When the intestines finally fail to respond to even the stronger laxatives, the result is not a cure for constipation but a chronic condition. The excessive stimulation causes inactivity of the local tissues, muscles and nerves. The use of saline purges has a different effect. A saline solution passed through the intestinal tract draws from the lymph stream large quantities of fluid which will usually be found to be excessively acid or loaded with poison from body waste. Unless this acid, toxic or poisoned lymph so expelled is replaced by an organic alkaline solution such as natural raw fruit juices, the final result is an inevitable deficiency in the body. In addition, if this replacement or realkalinization is not taken care of then, in the natural course of events, poisons remaining in the intestinal tact will, by being reabsorbed, find their way into the lymph stream and aggravate the original condition.

Raw spinach juice is Nature's way for the cleansing, regeneration and reconstruction of the intestinal tract. Raw spinach juice, combined with equal parts of apple juice, taken at the rate of about one pint daily has often corrected the most aggravated case of constipation within a few days or weeks.

Contrary to popular belief, it's not primarily the mechanical stimulus of "roughage" which favors bowel function. Rather, it is the *chemical* stimuli resulting from the fermentation of hemicellulose and cellulose (undigestible food residues) by intestinal bacteria. Hemicellulose is also most important in increasing the bulk of the stool. Foods with a high hemicellulose content are therefore definitely laxative. Spinach is a good example of this; apple is another. That is why a combination of the two is so effective even in the most severe cases of constipation.

As spinach works by natural means to repair the most essential damage first, it is not at first obvious that the work of regeneration is progressing. Results may not be noticeable for perhaps six weeks or two months of daily consumption of this juice. The bowels must be cleared at least once in every twenty-four hours during this period, therefore the most effective laxative the individual has found should be used and gradually reduced as the bowel movements become normal.

Raw spinach juice is also effective for the teeth and gums in preventing pyorrhea. This disease is a mild form of scurvy and results from a deficiency in the body of the elements found particularly in the combination of carrot and spinach juices. Bleeding gums and a fibroid degeneration of the pulp of the teeth has become a common defect due to the habitual use of devitalized cereals, refined sugar and other deficiency foods.

One word of caution: spinach contains a large amount of oxalic acid which combines with its calcium content, making most of the latter unavailable to the body and forming calcium oxalate. (Because of spinach's high calcium content, however, it's unlikely that its oxalic acid would have to combine with any of the body calcium.) Normally, calcium oxalate, an unassimilable salt, is passed *in solution* (dissolved) in the urine. In some cases, because of an unknown disturbance of kidney metabolism, the kidneys are unable to dissolve these salts and calcium oxalate crystals are precipitated in the urine, a condition known as oxaluria. These crystals form a large part of most kidney stones. Those who suffer from oxaluria or have a history of kidney stones, therefore, should avoid spinach as well as all the other foods (potatoes, beans, endives, tomatoes, dried figs, plums, strawberries, cocoa, chocolate and tea) which are high in oxalates. In addition, because of its potency, spinach should never be taken alone but in combination with other juices.

PARSLEY JUICE should never be taken in quantities of more than two ounces at a time, unless mixed with a sufficient quantity of carrot or other raw vegetable juices such as celery, lettuce or spinach, and even then in a smaller proportion than the other juices.

The elements in parsley help to maintain the blood vessels, particularly the capillaries and arterioles in a healthy condition. These elements are essential to oxygen metabolism in maintaining the normal action of the adrenal and thyroid glands. Being an excellent food for the genitourinary tract, it is of great assistance in conditions of calculi in the kidneys and bladder, albuminuria, nephritis and other kidney troubles.

Raw parsley juice mixed with carrot juice and with carrot and celery juices is efficient in every ailment connected with the eyes and optic nerve system, and will benefit weak eyes, ulceration of the cornea, cataracts, conjunctivitis, ophthalmia or laziness of the pupil.

Raw parsley juice is extremely potent and should never be drunk in great quantity by itself, for its high concentration will result in disarrangement of the nervous system. Taken with other juices properly mixed, it is very beneficial.

TURNIP LEAVES contain the most calcium of all vegetables, having more than one-half calcium. It is an excellent food for growing children and for anyone having softening of the bones in any shape or form, including the teeth. The combination of turnip leaves juice with carrot and dandelion juice is one of the most effective means of hardening the teeth as well as the entire bone structure of the body. The high magnesium content of the dandelion together with the calcium in the turnip leaves and the elements of the carrot combine to give this firmness and strength.

Turnip leaves also have a high potassium content which makes it a strong alkalinizer, particularly when combined with celery and carrot juices, and is excellent in reducing hyperacidity. Turnip leaves also contain much sodium and iron.

WATERCRESS JUICE is exceedingly high in sulphur which represents more than one-third of all the other minerals and salts combined in the watercress. Nearly forty-five per cent of the elements in watercress are acid forming, including sulphur, phosphorus and chlorine. As it is a very powerful intestinal cleanser, it should never be taken alone, but used with other juices such as carrot or celery.

Of the alkaline elements in watercress juice, there is potassium which is slightly more than 20%, calcium about 18%, sodium 8%, magnesium 5%, iron about one fourth of one percent.

A combination of carrot juice and spinach with some lettuce, turnip leaves and watercress juice is excellent for low blood pressure, underweight and anemia.

A combination of carrot, spinach, turnips and watercress has been known to act upon hemorrhoids or piles and many kinds of tumors. Two pints of this combination taken daily plus the elimination of all flour and sugar products and meat from the diet have been found to dissolve these conditions in from one to six months, provided there has been no surgical interference, in which event it may take longer.

CUCUMBER JUICE is probably the best natural diuretic known, secreting and promoting the flow of urine. It also aids in the promotion of hair growth, due to its high silicon and sulphur content, particularly when mixed with carrot, lettuce and spinach juice. It contains more than 40% potassium, 10% sodium, 7½% calcium, 20% phosphorus and 7% chlorine.

Cucumber juice added to carrot juice is beneficial in rheumatic ailments resulting from an excessive retention of uric acid in the system. Beet juice added to this combination speeds up the general process.

DANDELION JUICE is a valuable tonic. It is useful in counteracting hyperacidity and in normalizing the alkalinity of the system. It is our richest food in magnesium content and is high in potassium, calcium and sodium.

Magnesium gives firmness to the skeleton and prevents softening of the bones. A sufficient quantity of magnesium and calcium in the food during pregnancy will prevent the loss or degeneration of teeth due to childbirth and give firmness and strength to the bones of the child.

Organic magnesium in proper combination with calcium, iron and sulphur is essential in the formation of certain ingredients of the blood and is thus a great vitalizing force.

Organic magnesium can only be obtained from live fresh plants and must be used fresh and raw. It must not be confused with manufactured magnesium preparations which as inorganic minerals interfere with the proper healthy functions of the body.

Raw dandelion juice obtained from the leaves and combined with carrot and turnip leaves juice will assist in remedying spinal and other bone ailments, as well as give strength and firmness to the teeth, thus helping to prevent pyorrhea and decay.

FENNEL JUICE is somewhat like celery, a little sweeter and with an aromatic impression of licorice. It is also known as anise and by the Italians as finocchio.

Its value as food for the entire optic system is great, it is rich in all the most valuable elements and vitamins, and, when mixed with carrot juice, is a great aid in cases of night blindness and other eye troubles.

TOMATO JUICE is very rich in all the most vital elements required to neutralize an excessively acid condition of the body as a result of eating much concentrated starches and meats. Tomato juice should not be taken during the same meal where any starch or sugar is included, as these will neutralize its alkaline reaction. When taken alone, however, or during meals in which no starches or sugar are included, it is then beneficial as a natural alkalizer. Benzoate of soda added to tomato juice is harmful.

STRING BEANS AND BRUSSEL SPROUTS furnish a natural insulin for the pancreatic functions of the digestive organism. Diabetics who eliminate sugars and starches of every kind and who drink a combination of the juices of carrot, lettuce, string beans and Brussels sprouts, will be greatly benefited.

ONION AND GARLIC: Onion juice is helpful for nervousness, insomnia, and rheumatism. It is a good blood purifier and helpful in nose and throat infections as it helps kill bacteria.

Garlic may not help you to win friends and influence people, but it is a fine blood purifier. It is an absorber of uric acid and is useful in cases of high blood pressure. It has proven helpful in diseases of lungs and bronchi. Eating parsley at the same time will greatly lessen the odour.

APPLE AND CARROT: An aid in jaundice, gastric catarrh, arthritis, neuritis, cystitis, skin eruption, constipation and sluggish liver.

CARROT AND COCOANUT: A good supply of calcium, magnesium and iron. This combination is excellent as a body builder and has a perfect balance in its action and reaction on the human system. Good for peptic ulcers.

CELERY AND LEMON: An excellent neutralizer of digestion gases if taken before food is eaten. High in sodium content and serves as a tonic for nerve relaxation.

CARROT, CELERY, SPINACH AND PARSLEY: Rich in potassium, this food combination embraces practically the entire range of organic minerals and salts. If taken raw the potassium broth is excellent food for both young and old.

Mixed half and half with orange juice it is excellent as a stomach sweetener upon arising in the morning.

CABBAGE, CUCUMBER AND GRAPEFRUIT: Has chlorine and sulphur properties, a combination which is especially good for cleansing of the mucous membranes of the stomach and intestinal tract. Recognized as being the best natural diuretic known. A natural antiseptic. Should not be taken in cases of colitis.

CARROT, BEET AND COCOANUT: In this combination a food is obtained which in addition to its properties as an intensive body builder has even more potent qualities as a cleanser of the kidneys and gall bladder. Contains the alkaline elements potassium, sodium, calcium, magnesium and iron in abundance.

CARROT, BEET AND CUCUMBER: This preparation is one of the finest cleansing and healing materials for the gall bladder, the kidneys and glands.

CARROT, CELERY, ENDIVE AND PARSLEY: Rich in vital minerals—contains iron, sodium and calcium. Excellent in cases of asthma, skin disease, biliousness, poor blood, gall stones and gall bladder irritation, diseases of the urinary tract, stomach ulcers, inflammation of middle ear and for general body building.

CARROT, APPLE AND BEET TOP: Rich source of iron and other minerals. Valuable in cases of anemia, constipation, arthritis, bad blood, obesity, tumors, pimples and low vitality.

CARROT, CELERY AND TURNIP LEAVES: Rich in minerals and indicated for anemia, acidosis, impure blood, tumors, high blood pressure, poor appetite, bladder disorder and torpid liver. Especially good for its high calcium content.

CARROT, DANDELION AND LETTUCE: Good for poor appetite, nerve tonic and a mild diuretic. Excellent for colds, rheumatism, arthritis, kidney, bladder and liver disorders. A good blood cleanser and body purifier. High in its magnesium content.

CARROT, SPINACH & ORANGE: A vital food for the entire digestive tract, both the alimentary section of the body (the stomach, duodenum and small intestines) and for the large intestines or colon. Very acceptable to the taste. High iron content.

CELERY, TOMATO AND RADISH: A natural antiseptic. A protection against infection, sinus congestion and aids in obesity, catarrh, constipation, gall stones, kidney disorders, nerve exhaustion and is slightly diuretic.

SPINACH, WATERCRESS AND ORANGE: Exceedingly high in iron and sulphur content. Serves as an excellent intestinal cleanser. Combination affords a good supply of vitamin C and E.

PINEAPPLE AND CUCUMBER: A mild, natural digestive stimulant and a good general gland regulator. Slightly diuretic and especially goor for ulcers of the stomach, kidney stones and bladder disorder.

PINEAPPLE: Contains papain a valuable digestive, rich in chlorine which aids in digestion of proteins. Good for sore throat and bronchitis and in cases of diphtheria.

ORANGE: Especially good as a blood cleanser, has a rapid alkaline effect on an over-acid condition of the body. Rich in Vitamins A, B and C.

GRAPEFRUIT: Rich in fruit acids and sugars and if used naturally has an alkaline reaction in the body. Valuable as an aid in the removal or dissolving of inorganic calcium deposits formed in the cartilage of the joints as in arthritis.

BLUEBERRY AND HUCKLEBERRY: A natural astringent, a good blood purifier and an antiseptic. Indicated in cases of dysentery, acidosis, high blood pressure, menstruation disorders and diabetes.

STRAWBERRY, CHERRY, PRUNE AND DATE: Alkalizing in its general effect, slightly laxative and a concentrated body nourishment for those low in vitality. Especially good for those with low blood pressure, poor circulation, nervousness and weak stomachs.

STRAWBERRY AND DATE: One of the best skin-cleansing foods known. Indicated in cases of sluggish skin, poor complexion, pimples, acne, ring worm, sore eyes, sore throat and quinsy.

PAPAYA PULP, LEMON JUICE WITH DEXTROSE AND LACTOSE: Contains large amount of papain or vegetable pepsin, valuable in various digestive disturbances. Especially good for sensitive stomachs, a wonderful tonic in its rebuilding effect on the stomach and digestive tract. Sweetening agent good for its influence in changing the intestinal flora.

STRAWBERRY AND COCOANUT: Neutral in its general effect, this combination makes a generally good body-builder. Soothing in cases of sore throat, stomach ulcers and gastritis.

Recommended at The Juice Jug Cafe:

FOR THE HEART

Grape juice is the ideal beverage for all heart complaints; it nourishes and strengthens.

Pear juice stirs the kidneys to work, promotes the excretion of water, and assists heart activity in this way. Taken at time of midday nap or night rest, it is especially effective. The body uses bedrest in order to eliminate more water.

The greatest achievement of "Nature Cure Philosophy"
lies in the fact that it has reduced
the treatment of acute and sub-acute diseases,
as well as of chronic ailments,
to the greatest simplicity.

Dr. Henry Lindlahr

6. Formulas for Specific Ailments

In our preceding chapters we discussed the juice combinations and their action on the human body.

We will now list various juice formulas that will be of benefit to specific diseases.

The use of cabbage juice for the treatment of ulcers is one of the latest and most vital advances in the field of juice therapy. The healing agent, Vitamin U, was isolated and identified by Dr. Garnett Cheney of the Stanford University School of Medicine.

The treatment consisted of the addition of a quart of cabbage juice to the daily diet, taken five times a day in six-ounce quantities.

The anti-ulcer factor, vitamin U, is destroyed by cooking. Therefore in the tests Dr. Cheney made with patients, no other raw food was permitted. This proved that fresh cabbage juice alone, transmitted the healing units of Vitamin U. The therapeutic effect of the treatment was shown periodically by X-ray examinations.

Cabbage juice may also be of value in a preventative role where persons are either prone to an ulcerated condition or want to prevent a recurrence of this condition.

As celery juice also contains vitamin U, the combination of cabbage and celery juices (half-and-half) is also beneficial in ulcer treatment.

The person who seriously suffers from one or a combination of diseases must first go on a liquid diet completely for a few days, with daily enemas or a herb laxative to clear the bowels. From then on, his diet must be strictly fruits and vegetables with starch and protein added gradually as his condition improves.

The following juices are too potent to be used alone and should always be combined with other juices: beet, beet greens, spinach, parsley, dandelion, garlic, asparagus, lemon (always dilute with water), watercress, turnip.

Ailments and Juice Formulas

At least 16 ounces of juices are recommended daily. Each individual may choose the juice formula he likes best or he may vary it from day to day using anyone of the formulas specified under the particular ailment. In all cases, the formulas should be made up of the pure, raw juices as they come, undiluted, from the juicer.

ACNE, PIMPLES, ETC: Caused by impurities which the body
is trying to eliminate through the skin.
Juice combinations:
Carrot juice alone
Carrot 10 ounces, spinach 6 ounces
Carrot 8 oz., lettuce 5 oz., spinach 3 oz.

ADENOIDS: Inflammation or enlargement of pharyngeal tonsil or adenoid tissue. Juice combinations are:
Carrot juice alone
Carrot 10 ounces, spinach 6 ounces

ALBUMINURIA: Albumin in the urine. Juice combinations:
Carrot 10 ounces, spinach 6 ounces
Carrot 10 oz., beet 3 oz., cucumber 3 oz.
Carrot 11 oz., beet 3 oz., cocoanut 2 oz.
Carrot 9 ounces, celery 5 ounces, parsley 2 ounces
Carrot 12 ounces, parsley 4 ounces.

ALLERGIES: Sensitiveness to certain foods, pollens, or other substances of plants, insect bites, dust, etc., which may produce hay fever, nettle-rash, asthma, eczema, dyspepsia and headache. Juice combinations which help to keep the mucous membrane healthy and build resistance to disease are:
Carrot 6 oz., beet 5 oz., cucumber 5 oz.
Carrot 8 ounces, celery 8 ounces.

ANEMIA: Impoverishment in quantity and quality of the red corpuscles of fluid in the blood.
Juice combinations:
Carrot 12 ounces, spinach 4 ounces
Carrot 8 ounces, celery 6 ounces, beet 2 ounces
Carrot 6 ounces, beet 5 ounces, cucumber 5 ounces
Carrot 8 ounces, celery 4 ounces, spinach 2 ounces, parsley 2 ounces

ANGINA PECTORIS: Valvular or muscular heart trouble resulting from impurities in the blood stream.
Juice combinations:
Carrot 12 ounces, spinach 4 ounces
Carrot 6 oz., beet 5 oz., cucumber 5 oz.
Carrot 8 ounces, celery 4 ounces, spinach 2

ounces, parsley 2 ounces

Parsley should be used often as a garnish for meat dishes and ground horseradish (not juice) should be used as a sauce.

ARTERIES, (Hardening of): Thickening of the artery walls, causing a partial blocking of the blood stream to one or more organs due to presence of inorganic calcium.

Juice combinations:

Carrot 10 ounces, spinach 6 ounces

Carrot 8 ounces, celery 4 ounces, beet 4 ounces

Carrot 8 ounces, celery 4 ounces, spinach 2 ounces parsley 2 ounces

Carrot 8 ounces, garlic 2 ounces, pineapple 6 ounces

ARTHRITIS: Deposits of inorganic calcium in the cartilage of the joints as a result of eating concentrated carbohydrates in excess.

Juice combinations:

Carrot 8 ounces, celery 8 ounces

Carrot 6 ounces, beet 5 ounces, cucumber 5 ounces

(During acute stage—1 pint to 1 quart celery juice daily)

(Grapefruit juice is also helpful for those who find it doesn't aggravate their condition).

ASTHMA: Extreme difficulty in breathing due to mucous accumulation in bronchial tubes.

Juice combinations:

Carrot 10 ounces, spinach 6 ounces

Grapefruit

Carrot 8 ounces, celery 8 ounces

ASTIGMATISM: An error of refraction in the eye due to the cornea (the clear membrane in front of the eye) being unequally curved in different directions, so that rays of light in different meridians cannot be brought to a focus together in the retina.

Juice combinations:

Carrot 8 ounces, celery 8 ounces

Carrot 6 ounces, beet 5 ounces, cucumber 5 ounces

Carrot 8 ounces, celery 6 ounces, parsley 2 ounces

Carrot 12 ounces, spinach 4 ounces

BAD BREATH: Usually caused by constipation, indigestion, chronic tonsilitis, diseases of the nose, decayed or ulcerated teeth.

Juice combinations:

Juice of ½ lemon in glass of warm water in the morning, then:

Carrot 8 ounces, celery 8 ounces

Carrot 8 ounces, spinach 4 ounces, cucumber 4 ounces

BILIOUSNESS: The result of incomplete digestion of fats causing improper secretion and flow of bile from the liver.

Juice combinations:

Carrot 10 ounces, spinach 6 ounces

Carrot 10 ounces, cucumber 3 ounces, beet 3 ounces

Carrot 9 ounces, celery 5 ounces, parsley 2 ounces

BLADDER DISEASE: This includes gallstones or sand in the gallbladder, inflammation of the urinary bladder.

Juice combinations:

Carrot 6 ounces, beet 5 ounces, cucumber 5 ounces

Carrot 8 ounces, celery 4 ounces, spinach 2 ounces, parsley 2 ounces

BLOOD PRESSURE: *High blood pressure* is excessive tension of blood in the arteries caused by improper diet, lack of exercise and to a lesser extent by neurasthenia, worry, anxiety.

Low blood pressure is due to excessive use of devitalized foods in the diet, resulting in deficiency of vital elements in the blood stream. It frequently is the result of exhaustion, weakening disease, fevers and, generally, diseases of the heart.

Juice combinations:

Carrot 12 ounces, spinach 4 ounces

Carrot 6 ounces, beet 5 ounces, cucumber 5 ounces

Carrot 8 ounces, celery 4 ounces, spinach 2 ounces, parsley 2 ounces

(For high blood pressure only. Run one pod of garlic through juicer first; then run enough carrots to make 8 ounces of juice. Limit—8 ounces, once per day. Have a weekly check-up with your doctor.)

BOILS, CARBUNCLES: Purulent tumors caused by impurities in the blood stream resulting in bacterial infection through the sweat glands or the follicles of the hair.

Juice combinations:

Carrot 12 ounces, spinach 4 ounces

Carrot 6 ounces, beet 5 ounces, cucumber 5 ounces

Carrot 10 ounces, beet 3 ounces, cucumber 3 ounces

Carrot 8 ounces, lettuce 5 ounces, spinach 3 ounces

BRIGHTS DISEASE: Disease of the kidneys characterized by albumin in the urine, sometimes involving dropsy. Excessive uric acid.

Juice combinations:

Carrot 6 ounces, beet 5 ounces, cucumber 5 ounces

Carrot 12 ounces, spinach 4 ounces

Carrot 8 ounces, celery 6 ounces, parsley 2 ounces

BRONCHITIS: Inflammation of the bronchial tubes due to excessive mucus in the system.

Juice combinations:

Carrot 12 ounces, spinach 4 ounces

Carrot 8 ounces, celery 8 ounces

Carrot 6 ounces, beet 5 ounces, cucumber 5 ounces

CANCER: A malignant form of tumor; groups or nests of epithelial cells, half-starved from lack of proper organic nourishment, thriving on concentrated starches and meats.

Juice combinations:

Carrot (a quart a day is frequently taken with beneficial results)

Carrot 8 ounces, celery 8 ounces

Carrot 12 ounces, spinach 4 ounces

Carrot 12 ounces, cabbage 4 ounces

(It is important to have careful guidance under

the supervision of an experienced physician.)

CATARACTS: Opaque films over crystalline lens of the eye due to lack of proper nourishment to optic nerves and muscles.

Juice combinations:

Carrot 8 ounces, celery 6 ounces, parsley 2 ounces

Carrot 6 ounces, beet 5 ounces, cucumber 5 ounces

Carrot 12 ounces, spinach 4 ounces

Carrot 12 ounces, spinach 2 ounces, parsley 2 ounces

CATARRH: Copious secretion from the mucous membranes due to the inability of the body to assimilate properly milk and concentrated starches.

Juice combinations:

Carrot 8 ounces, celery 8 ounces

Carrot 12 ounces, spinach 4 ounces

Carrot 6 ounces, beet 5 ounces, cucumber 5 ounces

COLDS: Usually the result of low resistance to infection. Deficiency in vitamins and minerals is the causative factor; wet feet, inadequate clothing when exposed to cold, careless habits of elimination, fatigue.

Juice combinations are the same as for catarrh.

COLITIS: Inflammation of the colon (first part of the large intestine). Most prominent symptom is passage of mucus with the stools, with alternate periods of constipation and diarrhea. Unbalanced diet and inadequate vitamins and minerals are causative factors. Juice of ½ lemon in glass of warm water in morning; then,

Juice combinations:

Carrot 8 ounces, apple 8 ounces

Carrot 6 ounces, beet 5 ounces, cucumber 5 ounces

CONSTIPATION: Lack of co-ordination in the nerve and muscle functions of the colon and bowel due to excessive use of devitalized foods in the diet, resulting in sluggishness of bowel action.

Juice of ½ lemon in glass of warm water in morning; then:

Juice combinations:

Carrot 8 ounces, apple 8 ounces

Carrot 8 ounces, celery 4 ounces, apple 4 ounces

Carrot 12 ounces, spinach 4 ounces

CORONARY THROMBOSIS: When the coronary arteries are diseased they may become so narrow that the blood, slowing down its flow, clots or forms thrombosis. This cuts off the supply of blood to part of the heart and the result may be fatal.

Juice combinations:

Carrot 8 ounces, garlic 2 ounces (see page 86, blood pressure)

Carrot 8 ounces, parsley 2 ounces

Carrot 6 ounces, beet 5 ounces, cucumber 5 ounces

(Ground horseradish—not juice—up to one tablespoonful, used as sauce for meat.)

DERMATITIS: Inflammation of the skin—especially where the cuticle comes off in large flakes, leaving red surface beneath. Deficiency in vitamin A and panthothenic acid and some other vitamins and minerals.

Juice combinations:

Carrot 8 ounces, celery 8 ounces

Carrot 6 ounces, celery 5 ounces, apple 5 ounces

Carrot 6 ounces, celery 5 ounces, beet 5 ounces

Carrot 6 ounces, beet 5 ounces, cucumber 5 ounces

DIABETES: Inability of the pancreas to metabolize carbohydrates due to excessive use of concentrated starches and sugars in the diet.

Juice combinations:

Carrot 10 ounces, spinach 6 ounces

Carrot 7 ounces, celery 4 ounces, parsley 2 ounces, spinach 3 ounces

Carrots 6 ounces, lettuce 4 ounces, string bean 3 ounces, Brussel sprouts 3 ounces

Carrot 7 ounces, celery 5 ounces, endive (escarole) 2 ounces, parsley 2 ounces

DIARRHEA: Usually is a symptom of some disease situated in the intestines which causes looseness of bowels.

Juice combinations:

Carrot 8 ounces, apple 8 ounces

Carrot 6 ounces, celery 5 ounces, apple 5 ounces

Carrot 6 ounces, celery 6 ounces, spinach 2 ounces, parsley 2 ounces

EYE DISEASES: Frequently due to eye strain, poor light, glare — deficiency of vitamin A and other vitamins-minerals.

Juice combinations:

Carrot 12 ounces, spinach 4 ounces

Carrot 8 ounces, celery 8 ounces

Carrot 8 ounces, celery 6 ounces, spinach 2 ounces

FEVER: Abnormal increase in temperature. A common accompaniment of disease in general.

Choice of: citrus, apple, pineapple, grape, carrot, celery.

GALLSTONES: Pigments deposited from the bile in the finer vessels produce bile-sand. This bile sand may collect into small masses in the larger duct or gall bladder, and chemical changes in the mucous take place, so that a large gallstone may be produced. Unbalanced diet is a causative factor. (Avoid fatty, spiced, starchy, too heavily salted foods.) Juice of ½ lemon in glass of warm water in morning, then:

Juice combinations:

Carrot 8 ounces, celery 8 ounces

Carrot 6 ounces, beet 5 ounces, cucumber 5 ounces (preferable)

GOITER: Enlargement of the thyroid gland due to lack of organic iodine in the diet. Add ¼ teaspoon of Powdered Kelp or Dulse to each formula.

Juice combinations:

Carrot 12 ounces, spinach 4 ounces

Carrot 8 ounces, celery 8 ounces

Carrot 8 ounces, celery 6 ounces, spinach 2 ounces, parsley 2 ounces

GOUT: Inflammation of the ligaments of a joint or bone, or bone lining, due to excessive fat in the diet, also due to excessive use of alcohol and other stimulants, which cause excess uric acid in the blood.

Juice combinations:

Potassium broth (Carrot 8 ounces, celery 4 ounces, spinach 2 ounces, parsley 2 ounces)

Carrot 8 ounces, spinach 8 ounces

Carrot 6 ounces, beet 5 ounces, cucumber 5 ounces

Carrot 8 ounces, beet 4 ounces, cocoanut 4 ounces

HAY FEVER: Abnormal mucous secretions in the eyes and air passages, due to excessive use of starches in the diet.

Juice combinations:

Carrot 8 ounces, celery 8 ounces

Carrot 6 ounces, beet 5 ounces, cucumber 5 ounces

Carrot 8 ounces, celery 4 ounces, spinach 2 ounces, parsley 2 ounces

HEADACHES: (Chronic) Nature's warning to give the body a thorough house cleaning, thus re-establishing the equilibrium of the blood and releasing its excessive pressure in the regions of the head

Juice combinations:

Carrot 10 ounces, spinach 6 ounces

Carrot 7 ounces, celery 4 ounces, parsley 2 ounces, spinach 3 ounces

Carrot 10 ounces, beet 3 ounces, cucumber 3 ounces

Carrot 8 ounces, lettuce 5 ounces, spinach 3 ounces

HEART TROUBLE: (Functional) Caused by the impure condition of the blood resulting in improper activity on the part of the heart organism.

Juice combinations:

Carrot 10 ounces, spinach 6 ounces

Carrot 7 ounces, celery 4 ounces, parsley 2 ounces, spinach 3 ounces

Carrot 10 ounces, beet 3 ounces, cucumber 3 ounces

HEMORRHOIDS: Consists of varicose veins and often an in-
(Piles) flammed condition of the veins about the lower part of the bowel.

Juice combinations:

Carrot 12 ounces, spinach 4 ounces

Carrot 8 ounces, spinach 2 ounces, celery 4 ounces, parsley 2 ounces

Carrot 8 ounces, watercress 8 ounces

(For seven days, chop one apple (with skin on, but remove core), mix apple pulp with cream— eat as a sauce for breakfast. Then, alternate every other day with apple juice for breakfast. The chopped-apple-and-cream supplies bulk and has healing qualities.)

HERNIA: Protrusion of any internal organ wholly or in part from its normal position, due to lack of tone in the surrounding membranes.

Juice combinations:

Carrot 12 ounces, spinach 4 ounces

Carrot 6 ounces, celery 6 ounces, spinach 2 ounces, parsley 2 ounces

Carrot 8 ounces, celery 8 ounces

INFLUENZA: Caused by excessive retention in the system of

body and food waste resulting in a feeding and breeding ground for pathogenic bacteria, affecting principally the air passages but accompanied by fever, nervous prostration, mental depression, followed by great debility.

Juice combinations:

Carrot 8 ounces, celery 8 ounces

Carrot 12 ounces, spinach 4 ounces

Carrot 6 ounces, beet 5 ounces, cucumber 5 ounces

INSOMNIA: Inability to sleep as a result of nervous tension or excessive acidity in the system.

Juice combinations:

Carrot 10 ounces, spinach 6 ounces

Carrot 8 ounces, celery 7 ounces

(If celery tops—greens—are used, then change the proportion to 10 ounces carrot, 6 ounces celery.)

JAUNDICE: The result of an overburdened liver eliminating the excretion of bile by way of the lymph stream through the pores of the skin.

Juice combinations:

Juice of ½ lemon in glass of warm water in morning, then:

Carrot 10 ounces (preferable, to insure taking ample vitamin A)

Carrot 8 ounces, celery 6 ounces, parsley 2 ounces

Carrot 6 ounces, beet 5 ounces, cucumber 5 ounces

KIDNEY DISEASES. (Excessive Uric Acid, etc.) The result of

improper and insufficient elimination of the end product of excessive use of meat in the diet.

Juice combinations:

Juice of ½ lemon in glass of warm water in morning, then:

Carrot 12 ounces, spinach 4 ounces

Carrot 8 ounces, celery 8 ounces

Carrot 6 ounces, beet 5 ounces, cucumber 5 ounces

Carrot 8 ounces, celery 6 ounces, parsley 2 ounces

LARYNGITIS: Inflammation of the larynx due to the presence of morbid matter in the body.

Juice combinations:

Carrot 8 ounces, pineapple 8 ounces

Carrot 8 ounces, apple 8 ounces

Carrot 8 ounces, celery 8 ounces

Carrot 6 ounces, beet 5 ounces, cucumber 5 ounces

LIVER TROUBLE: The result of eating an excess of devitalized and concentrated starches, sugars, fats and meats.

Juice combinations:

Carrot 10 ounces, beet 3 ounces, cucumber 3 ounces

Carrot 10 ounces, spinach 6 ounces

Carrot 11 ounces, beet 3 ounces, cocoanut 2 ounces

MALAISE: Vague feeling of feverishness, listlessness and fatigue, which often precedes the onset of serious acute disease, or accompanies disorders such as cold, chills or dyspepsia. General run-down condition. Deficiency in vitamins and minerals a causative factor.

Juice combinations:

Carrot 8 ounces, celery 8 ounces

Carrot 8 ounces, apple 8 ounces

Carrot 6 ounces, beet 5 ounces, cucumber 5 ounces

MIGRAINE: Impure blood stream and improperly nourished nerve centers causing intense ache, usually on one side only of the head, dulling and depressing the individual.

Juice combinations:

Carrot 10 ounces, spinach 6 ounces

Carrot 7 ounces, celery 4 ounces, parsley 2 ounces, spinach 3 ounces

Carrot 10 ounces, beet 3 ounces, cucumber 3 ounces

MUCOUS MEMBRANE: Mucous membranes line all the cavities in the body and are lubricated by mucus derived usually from the glands or in some cases from isolated cells on the surface of the membrane. Adequate intake of vitamins and minerals *daily* is essential to maintain the mucous membranes in optimum health.

Juice combinations:

Carrot 8 ounces, apple 8 ounces

Carrot 8 ounces, pineapple 8 ounces

Carrot 8 ounces, celery 8 ounces

Carrot 6 ounces, beet 5 ounces, cucumber 5 ounces

NEPHROSIS: General term applied to any disease of the kidneys, but especially to a form of degeneration characterized by anemia, widespread dropsy and a high degree of albuminuria.

Juice combinations:

Carrot 12 ounces, spinach 4 ounces

Carrot 8 ounces, celery 6 ounces, parsley 2 ounces

Carrot 6 ounces, beet 5 ounces, cucumber 5 ounces

NERVOUS SYSTEM: (Diseases of) Including such disorders as hysteria, forgetfulness, nerve injuries, neuralgia, neuritis, neurasthenia, diseases of the spinal cord, etc. General health should be built up and if possible, the cause of nervous tension removed.

Juice combinations:

Carrot 8 ounces, celery 8 ounces

Carrot 6 ounces, beet 5 ounces, cucumber 5 ounces

Carrot 8 ounces, celery 6 ounces, parsley 2 ounces

Carrot 12 ounces, spinach 4 ounces

(Celery juice is a nerve tonic. For best results, take after dinner or just before retiring.)

OPHTHALMIA: Also known as Conjunctivitis, Inflammation of the eye.

Juice combinations:

Carrot 8 ounces, celery 8 ounces

Carrot 8 ounces, apple 8 ounces

Carrot 12 ounces, spinach 4 ounces

Carrot 8 ounces, orange 8 ounces

OVERWEIGHT: A condition of the body characterized by over-accumulation of fat under the skin and around certain of the organs caused by an unbalanced diet.

Juice combinations:

Juice of ½ lemon in glass of warm water in morning; then;

Carrot 8 ounces, celery 8 ounces

Carrot 12 ounces, spinach 4 ounces

Carrot 6 ounces, beet 5 ounces, cucumber 5 ounces

PEPTIC ULCER: General term used for ulcers of the stomach and of the duodenum.

Juice combinations:

Cabbage 16 ounces, celery 16 ounces

A 6 ounce glass of cabbage juice five times a day.

PERNICIOUS ANEMIA: A severe form of anemia—poor quantity and quality of red corpuscles or fluid in the blood.

(See anemia for juice combinations)

PLEURISY: Inflammation of the pleura or serous membrane investing the lung and the inner surface lining of the rib.

Juice combinations:

Carrot 8 ounces, celery 8 ounces

Carrot 8 ounces, pineapple 8 ounces

Carrot 6 ounces, beet 5 ounces, cucumber 5 ounces

Carrot 8 ounces, celery 6 ounces, parsley 2 ounces

PREGNANCY: A balanced diet rich in vitamins and minerals are of especial importance during pregnancy and during the period of lactation.

Juice combinations:

Carrot 8 ounces, celery 4 ounces, coconut 4 ounces

Carrot 8 ounces, apple 8 ounces

Carrot 12 ounces, spinach 4 ounces

Carrot 8 ounces, orange 4 ounces, coconut 4 ounces

Carrot 6 ounces, beet 5 ounces, cucumber 5 ounces

PYELITIS: A condition of suppuration (formation of pus) in the kidneys, producing pus in the urine. It is due to inflammation of that part of the kidney known as the pelvis, which is connected with the ureter (a tube carrying urine from kidney to bladder). Pyelitis usually occurs along with inflammation of the bladder, with symptoms of feverishness, listlessness, loss of weight, discomfort and frequent passing of water.

Juice combinations:

Carrot 8 ounces, celery 8 ounces

Carrot 6 ounces, beet 5 ounces, cucumber 5 ounces

PYROSIS: (Heartburn) A symptom of dyspepsia consisting of an irritable, burning sensation in the throat, accompanied by constant secretion of saliva, caused by unbalanced diet and excess of fats, starches and spices in the diet.

Carrot 8 ounces, apple 8 ounces

Carrot 8 ounces, celery 8 ounces

Carrot 6 ounces, beet 5 ounces, cucumber 5 ounces

Carrot 12 ounces, spinach 2 ounces, parsley 2 ounces

RHEUMATISM: Many diseases are listed under this general heading; neuritis, sciatica, lumbago, arthritis, gout, etc.

These diseases are the result of an unbalanced diet which produces excessive morbid matter in the body.

Juice combinations:

Juice of ½ lemon in glass of warm water in morning, then:

Carrot 8 ounces, celery 8 ounces

Carrot 8 ounces, orange 8 ounces

Carrot 12 ounces, spinach 4 ounces

Carrot 6 ounces, beet 5 ounces, cucumber 5 ounces

Carrot 6 ounces, beet 5 ounces, celery 5 ounces

RHINITIS: Inflammation of the nasal membrane due to the presence of excessive quantities of mucus in the sinus cavities.

Juice combinations:

Carrot 8 ounces, celery 8 ounces (preferable)

Carrot 6 ounces, beet 5 ounces, cucumber 5 ounces

Carrot 6 ounces, celery 5 ounces, beet 5 ounces

RICKETS: Deficiency of organic calcium, all the vitamins and minerals, particularly vitamin D, causes softness and deformity of the bones.

Carrot 8 ounces, apples 8 ounces

Carrot 8 ounces, orange 8 ounces

Carrot 8 ounces, celery 8 ounces

Carrot 8 ounces, apple 6 ounces, spinach 2 ounces

SCURVY: A morbid condition of the blood and tissues

shown by marked impairment of the nutritive functions and by the occurrence of extravasations of blood in the tissues of the body. Caused by deficiency of vitamin C and other vitamins and minerals in the diet.

Juice combinations:

Oranges 8 ounces, grapefruit 8 ounces

Carrot 8 ounces, orange 8 ounces

Carrot 8 ounces, apple 8 ounces

Carrot 8 ounces, celery 8 ounces

SINUS TROUBLE: Usually due to excessive mucus resulting from excessive use of milk and, frequently, also of starches and sugars.

Juice combinations:

Carrot 10 ounces, spinach 6 ounces

Juice of 1 whole lemon, horseradish (ground, not pressed) 4 ounces

Carrot 10 ounces, beet 3 ounces, cucumber 3 ounces

TEETH: Nutrition plays an outstanding role in the development and maintenance of strong teeth. Calcium and phosphorus are needed in the daily diet plus the other vitamins and minerals.

Juice combinations:

Carrot 8 ounces, celery 8 ounces

Carrot 8 ounces, apple 8 ounces

Carrot 8 ounces, orange 8 ounces

Carrot 6 ounces, celery 5 ounces, beet 5 ounces

TONSILS: Two almond shaped glands, one on each side of the throat, covered with mucous membrane. Tonsilitis is inflammation of the tonsils and may be either acute or chronic. Deficiency of vitamins and minerals and an over-acid condition of the body are the cause of tonsilitis.

Juice combinations:

Carrot 8 ounces, pineapple 8 ounces

Carrot 8 ounces, orange 8 ounces

Carrot 8 ounces, apple 8 ounces

Carrot 8 ounces, celery 8 ounces

TUMORS: (In Bones) (In Liver) (In Uterus) Growths due to a lack of sufficient organic elements and caused by the excessive use of concentrated inorganic foods.

Juice combinations:

Carrot 8 ounces, beet 8 ounces (preferable)

Carrot 6 ounces, celery 6 ounces, parsley 2 ounces

Carrot 6 ounces, beet 5 ounces, cucumber 5 ounces

Carrot 8 ounces, celery 4 ounces, spinach 2 ounces, parsley 2 ounces

Watercress 8 ounces (twice daily)

VARICOSE VEINS: The result of diets rich in concentrated starches and sugars, which cause deposits to form in the wall structure of the veins (valves).

Juice combinations same as above.

For general health it is advisable to have either a 6 ounce glass of apple or orange juice in the morning, a 6 ounce glass of carrot juice in the mid-afternoon and a 6 ounce glass of celery juice before retiring. Do not have orange juice at bedtime. If a citrus fruit is preferred, have grapefruit juice, instead of celery juice.

Apple juice in the morning helps to regulate the functions of the body, to promote peristaltic activity and tones up the system for the day. In the afternoon, carrot juice or carrot combined with other juices, helps to keep the mucous membranes, cells, tissues, glands, bones, walls of the arteries, in fact the entire body in healthy condition. Celery juice or celery combined with other juices, before retiring is soothing, relaxing, alleviates anxiety and worry and promotes restful sleep.

THE JUICE JUG CAFE

In your mind's eye imagine a flower-lined promenade bordered by a fresh running brook on the left and delightful shops on the right side offering you all sorts of interesting items that do not conflict with your "cure" regimen. Then you come upon a flower-filled court yard opening between the shops and your eye is attracted to a good-sized quaint Tyrolean Chalet, its entrance lined with the usual sidewalk cafe type umbrella tables and chairs. The sun shines into this lovely scene from the South. The guests are all drinking from magnificent wine glasses, sparkling amber colored crystal, with flaring stems, brimming with fresh pressed carrot juice or other vegetable or fruit juices. The drinks are cooling and refreshing, but most of all, helping health, instead of hurting it, as most commonly used "refreshing" drinks do. To my mind, this "The Juice Jug Cafe" is the perfect "Juice Bar". Quoted here are some of the helpful hints contained in their menu:

FOR THE DIGESTION

"You always clear out a room before you renovate!" Apple juice left for one day to ferment, still has no alcoholic content and works excellently on the digestion. "It revolves in the barrel and the bowels but not in the head", says their proverb. Grape juice, left one day to ferment, builds up carbonic acid which combines with the grape sugar to produce a quickly noticeable stimulation and envigoration. This "hard" grape juice is more thoroughly cleansing than the "hard" apple juice.

FOR GOOD SLEEP

The best drink in the evening is warm Elder Berry juice. Do not drink any other juice either before or after Elder Berry. It works best that way. Elder Berry juice makes you tired, and quiets you. Taken just before going to bed it affords a deep natural sleep.

FOR THE LIVER, GALL, AND NERVES

Drinks straight out of the refrigerator, eating in haste and hurry, anger and excitement, all damage the gall, liver and nerves.

FOR BEAUTY, STRONG EYESIGHT, HAIR GROWTH, AND FOR GENERAL HEALTHY APPEARANCE

Taken before eating, carrot juice helps to prepare the digestive juices in the stomach and is very good for the gall and liver sufferer. Do not drink any fruit juice either just before or just after the carrot juice.

FOR LOW BLOOD PRESSURE

All juices from the dark fruits, black currents, Elderberry juice, dark grape juice, cherry juice, blackberry juice, bilberry juice.

> *"The vegetable juice idea ... in later years
> has become quite a commercial venture.
> Fast living today requires more concentrated
> and more easily assimilated foods.
> Consequently, the vegetable juice therapy
> has come into its own, and is served
> right on our street corners for our health's sake."*
>
> Dr. Bernard Jensen

7. The Mechanics of Raw Juice Extraction

The fruit and vegetable juicer market is large enough to present a challenge to the average consumer who has been "sold" on the raw juice cocktail hour. Which juicer to buy? Such a purchase usually represents a sizeable investment (from $70 to over $1200) for the family budget — though certainly one which pays off in big *healthy* dividends. Benjamin Franklin once said, "Empty your purse into your head." He meant that an education is your best and safest investment. I agree with him but feel compelled to add, "A purse emptied in building robust health is well spent."

When you have decided to make your investment in a juicer there are many factors to be considered. There are three or four basic types of juicers on the market, each with several brand names. You'll find that each brand has certain features or advantages over the others; similarly, each has particular disadvantage which the others do not. Some are meant to be used in hospitals and institutions; others are especially suitable for home use. You, as the consumer, must weigh all these pros and cons and decide which unit best fits your requirements in your individualized circumstances. To help you do this I will discuss briefly the different types of juicers and try to point out their various advantages and disadvantages. For more information, you can refer to the advertising pages of Nature's Path Magazine, P.O. Box 404, New York, NY 10156

To begin with, there are several things that all good juicers have in common and you as a prospective buyer should look for them in whichever juicer you are thinking of buying. All good juicers are made of non-corrodible, acid and alkali resistant material. In none of them does the food or juice come in contact with any aluminum parts. Thus you eliminate the possibility that any health-robbing aluminum compounds might contaminate the juice through chemical reaction. Any reliable manufacturer will give from three months to a year's guarantee on his juicer. (Any defect in the machine will have become obvious by then.) Now there are even five and ten year guarantees offered by manufacturers of high quality precision juicers. Naturally these guarantees do not cover damages or wear resulting from abuse, but they are guarantees that indicate the manufacturer's faith in the durability of his product.

In comparison to the old style methods, any electric juicer is able to extract a much higher percentage of the nutrients from the fruits and vegetables. Compare their performances with manually crushing and squeezing the pulp through a cheesecloth sieve. Or even with the efficiency of the hand juicer which looks very much like a tabletop meat grinder with a long snout through which the juice slowly trickles from a row of holes as you crank the handle.

The most popular type of electric juicer is the one designed to use the principle of centrifugal force. Basically, these juicers consist of a "feeder" or "hopper" into which the fresh fruit or vegetable is put, whole or cut up in pieces; a basket and cutter blade (which has jagged teeth) and mashes or "chews" into pulp the food that has been placed into it through the feeder and by whirling (the centrigual principle comes into play here), forces the juice through perforations in the side of the basket into the bowl surrounding it and out a spout into your waiting bottle or glass. Because the mashed pulp is retained in the spinning basket, a large percentage of the available juice can be extracted from the fruit or vegetable. (Note: Recent scientific tests indicate that the life-giving enzymes which are found in raw foods are *not* destroyed by this centrifugal process. Heating the food to temperatures of 140 degrees Farenheit is what destroys these healthful enzymes.) Usually after a pint or quart (depending on the juicer's size and power) has been extracted, the pulp should be removed to insure continued maximum production. This, then, is not the type of juicer which would be most helpful in a hospital or institution where large quantities of juice must be extracted before the requirements are filled. But it is the type that is well-suited to the average home.

A word of caution: Today there are a number of inexpensive food processors and blenders being sold with the implication that they are total juicers. Such machines are fortified blenders or shredders but do not and cannot extract juice from any fruit or vegetable. A juice extractor is the only type of machine that can do the job. Be sure you get the appliance that's right for your needs and don't be confused by misleading advertising.

Aside from the fact that many low-priced machines simply cannot be well-built, the main disadvantage is their smaller and slower rate of juice production. This makes them very expensive to use in the long run considering their inefficient extraction of juice. Invariably a weaker machine leaves more extractable juice in the pulp and too much pulp in the juice.

I suggest that if you are interested in experimenting with Raw Juice Therapy and you want to pay the least amount to begin with, examine the juicers selling in the $100 to $140 price range. In this group you will find some well-made machines both domestic and imported. But bear in mind that if you like what you learn you'll eventually "trade up" to one of the larger and better-built machines that is easier to use and clean, has sealed bearings, and a one-quart capacity.

Next in line would be the juicers which retail for around $200. In this group you will find machines made by experienced juicer manufacturers devoted solely to this field. For this price you can expect to get a machine made with all stainless steel juicing parts. It is in this repect that their higher cost is justified. *Look for a quiet ball-bearing motor, quick-release latch handles and assurance that you will get at least a quart of juice between pulp removals. They also should have a good quality cushion ring supporting the entire base to eliminate vibration and movement across the counter or table top.*

There is a top quality product in the juicer market with

which I am personally familiar. It is the elite of the market with spinner basket, cutting blade and bowl all made of pure stainless steel, a lid made of sturdy material, a powerful high speed electric motor reaching 3600 r.p.m., precision sealed bearings and flywheel acting as a gyroscope which helps keep up a constant speed no matter how quickly or slowly you feed the machine. This product sells for around $200. Here is why I consider the Omega Juicer to be the best and most economical machine to buy. Not only does it extract 30% more juice than most other leading brands, it's quality of workmanship and ease of operation make it,quick and easy to juice the nutritious fruits and vegetables that will reward you with better health. It is a fact that any machine which is difficult to use, clean, assemble or disassemble, will discourage you from using it often. I find the Omega Juicer to be a sheer joy to use. The teeth in the surgical stainless steel cutter blade are cut in under 100 tons of pressure per square inch. This "floating" cutter blade prevents the uneven accumulation of pulp within the basket and thus minimizes the vibration. The machine is extremely easy to clean. All elements lift apart without difficulty and no tools are ever required. I rate this machine tops for efficiency because it extracts the maximum juice from the fruit or vegetable, leaving the pulp dry. It does all this simply, quietly and swiftly. The American-made Omega Juicer is backed by a full ten year guarantee.

Most manufacturers provide books of instructions and recipes with each unit so you can start off on the right foot.

You will be surprised at the number and variety of nutritious juices which can be prepared.

A second *type* of electric juicer, the automatic pulp-ejector type, though also using the principle of centrifugal force, carries it one step further. Because of its parabolic-shaped spinner basket, the juice is passed out through the sides while the pulp is whirled over to the top into an exhaust spout. Though this permits long, continuous operation — it can make gallons of juice at a time, for the juicer does not have to be stopped to have the pump removed — it extracts a much lower percentage of the juice from the fruit or vegetable as compared with those machiens which retain the pulp in the spinner. Nutritionally it is most beneficial to drink juice immediately after extraction. Thus, the feature of making gallons of juice is not very beneficial to the average family.

During the past few years there have been a number of imported non-stop juicers promoted and sold in the U.S. They are different from the original domestic pulp-ejector types in that they are much smaller and lighter. Consequently, their production is slower and their plastic construction, although far superior to older plastic models, is still inferior to the expensive stainless steel models manufactured in the U.S.A. These range in price from a fair value of $70 to $130. Unfortunately the higher price often does not guarantee a better machine. Let the buyer beware!

Because a pulp-ejector type machine can be operated continuously, many people use it from one "juicing session" to the next without bothering to clean it. As a result, the fine holes of the strainer eventually become plugged with sediment and the machine does not function properly. The owner then ships it off to the manufacturer for "adjustment." The manufacturer finds that the only thing it needs is a thorough cleaning and tune up, however, he has to charge at least $25 to cover the shipping charges and labor. To avoid all this unnecessary expense and bother, the manufacturer advises you to wash the machine every day with some kind of detergent and a stiff brush, being careful to rinse well because some detergents also have a tendency to plug up the holes.

Another brand of pulp-ejector juicer, the Champion, is different from the rest in that it does not use the principle of centrifugal force. Instead, it seems to cut and then *grind* the fruit or vegetable which is fed to it and at the same time discard the pulp. It has a higher rate of extraction than the other automatic pulp-ejector juicers but it is still not higher than the type that keeps the pulp in the spinner. The pulp is expelled through the end of its spout while the juice is collected allowing continuous production. It is quiet and there is no air pressure blowing the pulp as there is with centrifugal pulp-ejectors. Only stainless steel and 100% Dupont Nylon touch the juice. This juicer has attachments to shred vegetables, make nut butter, baby food and homogenize. This latter feature can be a godsend for it will rapidly deseed tomatoes, berries, etc. A recipe book furnished with the Champion gives instructions on how to make nut butter, shaved ice, fresh fruit ice cream and baby food. It sells for around $240.

A third type of juicer uses hydraulic pressure for the actual extraction of the juice. Such as a juicer gets the largest percentage of liquid from the fruits and vegetables. The pulp is actually pressed dry. This juicer comes in two separate parts. The first part is a shredder which breaks the solid pieces down as small as possible. (This part can be used to shred fruits and vegetables for salads, desserts and soups; it can also be used to flake nuts and make nut butter.) The second part is actually a hydraulic press which takes the shredded fruit or vegetable and really ssqueezes all the juice out of it. What is left is only a dry sheet of fibers. This machine is very sturdily constructed and is capable of producing up to five gallons of juice in an hour. This is the Norwalk Juicer developed by Dr. Walker, a true pioneer of diet reform and raw juice therapy. It retails for over $1000.

The principle disadvantage of this kind of juicer is that the juice seems to have a mucher stronger taste. It is rather big and the two-step operation makes it impractical for the average home. It seems to be more suited for a nursing home or for the home of a chronic invalid where large quantities of juices are consumed so that its high rate of production and extraction is a definite advantage.

There are, no doubt, other brands of juicers on the market which haven't been described here. I hope though, that with the descriptions given, anyone interested in buying an electric juicer will be able to know what advantages and disadvantages to look for and will be able to judge accordingly.

Once you have made the investment and you proudly display in your kitchen the juicer which is best suited to your needs, the next step is to use it.

Many people think that with such an easy to use appliance, all there is to making fresh fruit or vegetable juice is to put any old thing in the juicer and catch it as it comes out. Life isn't quite as simple as that. There is an old axiom in chemistry which states that "matter can neither be created nor destroyed." You may change your food from one form to another but you can't increase it or make it any better without adding something else to it. Similarly, if you put over-ripe or bruised fruit or wilted vegetables in your juicer, you will get a poor quality juice. If you put in vital, organically-grown fruits or vegeables, you will get nutritious, delicious juice.

So, the first step in using your juicer properly is to select your fruits and vegetables with care. These should be crisp and fresh — preferably straight from your market. If neither of these two possibilities is practical, the next best thing to do is to store your fruits and vegetables in the refrigerator the minute they arrive from the market. These foods start losing their vitamin and mineral content as soon as they are picked because the life line is broken at that point. Refrigeration is the best means of retarding this deterioration process.

For this same reason, the fruit or vegetable should only be removed from the refrigerator just prior to making the juice. If at all possible, the juice should be made right before you drink it. Any juice that has been made and left standing, loses its vitamins and minerals quickly due to oxidation. Although these juices are refreshing and delicious to drink, the main reason we consume them is for their nutritional value.

When preparing the fruits and vegetables for juicing, be sure to cut out all the bruised or bad spots if there are any. These areas will only change the real color of the juice, encourage fermentation and hasten the loss of vitamins and minerals. Needless to say, all fruits and vegetables should be carefully washed before using — especially in this day and age of insecticides and chemical sprays. To do this, scrub the fruits and vegetables with a stiff vegetable brush under cold running water.

A good trick to remember is to squeeze a little lemon juice through the juicer before using it. This helps retain the original color of the fruit or vegetable and also helps to add more bioflavonoids to your diet.

All fruits and vegetables should be cut into pieces before placing in the feeder of the juicer. Many manufacturers claim that this is not necessary — that their particular juicer can take the fruit or vegetable whole. Nonetheless, for efficient operation and to obtain the maximum benefit from the foods, it is best to cut the food into pieces and thus take part of the load off the juicer. This, logically, should result in more efficient production and a longer-lasting juicer.

All manufacturers will include a printed set of instructions with their juicer which will tell you how best to clean it after using as well as how to operate it. But, regardless of the juicer, there are two important things to remember: *clean the juicer immediately after using and clean it thoroughly.* If you delay, the juicer will become clogged with the pulp and these dried fibers are difficult to remove at this stage. Chances are that then you won't clean the juicer really well. If the juicer is not cleaned thoroughly, the growth of bacteria is encouraged, fermentation is hastened and the next time around you will be losing vitamins and minerals. Some warm water and a stiff brush, put to work *immediately* after the juicer has been used, will avoid all this.

Most important of all, *use* the juicer — use it often. It is, perhaps, the only safe, sure and enjoyable way to make certain that you and your family are receiving adequate amounts of every one of the essential nutrients. It's good health insurance.

The secret of longevity
largely lies in eating intelligently.
Learn to like foods that are good for you.

Gayelord Hauser

8. Individualizing Your Menus

$\mathcal{Y}$OU HAVE YOUR juicer; you've "experimented" with it; you know now how to get the best production out of it. The question is, how do I start on this raw juice regime? It's really quite simple—once you know a few fundamental rules of good nutrition and you modify them to overcome your own deficiencies. (Remember these were a long time in the making and are not going to be corrected overnight.)

Here are a few good pointers to keep you on the straight and nutritious path:

1. Be sure to eat plenty of *raw* fruits and vegetables and their juices to insure an adequate intake of the essential vitamins and minerals.

2. Be sure you get your essential amino acids in one form of protein or another. (The essential amino acids are considered those which the body, itself, cannot manufacture and which, therefore, must come from an outside source, i.e., from the food we eat. They are arginine, histidine, isoleucine, leucine, lysine, methionine, phenylalanine, threon-

ine, tryptophane and valine.) You should not concentrate on getting one amino acid over the others for an imbalance of them can lead to a vitamin deficiency. (The body may need more than the normal amount of a particular vitamin to metabolize the surplus amino acid.) Eat the type of protein that is low in cholesterol but is as whole as possible. (Soybeans, and gluten, sesame seed and sunflower seeds are good examples of whole though nonflesh proteins.)

3.   Keep your carbohydrate intake low for, if you are getting an adequate supply of raw fruits and vegetables, part of your carbohydrate requirements will be met with the natural starches and sugars from these foods.

4.   Study the minimum daily requirements of the different nutrients, which have been drawn up by the National Research Council on Nutrition, and are given in the table on pages 144 to 146. Be sure that by the end of the day you've gotten more than your minimum daily requirements of vitamins and minerals. Remember that a body under stress—that is, when it is trying to ward off an invading disease, or when it is subjected to inclement weather—needs more than those "minimum" daily requirements to protect itself. If you will do this, you'll not be such an easy victim to the next visiting germ that comes aknocking at your door.

5.   In making up your minimum daily requirements remember that, in this day and age of devitalized, processed foods, chances are that the food that arrives at your home has already lost much of its nutritional value. Try to buy that food which is natural, which has not been ripened artificially, which has not had chemicals added to make it "look better" or to disguise its age much like an older wo-

man who hides behind cakes of powder and paint and is a sorry mess when stripped of her shield.

Try to eat as much raw food as possible for cooking further destroys whatever nutrients remain. For heaven's sake, don't deteriorate an already deteriorated situation by your cooking methods. Pressure cooking is the best—and, of course, the quickest—way of cooking. When food is cooked rapidly, the nutrients are locked in and do not escape in a cloud of vapor as is usually the case. I've often thought that if proper tests were made, we would find that the walls of the average kitchen are much more nutritiously fed than the inhabitants of the home.

Pressure cooking is not always within our means so, if you must cook the vegetables, by all means, steam them in a pot that has a tight-fitting, heavy cover. *Never use water when steaming vegetables.* Most vegetables have enough natural juices in them to insure that they will not burn. Besides this, the water which still clings to them from washing acts as another safeguard. Usually, no more liquid than this is necessary. Some vegetables, however, do take longer to release their juices than others. For these, a tablespoon or two of water at the bottom of the pot will suffice. Another helpful trick is to cook these vegetables along with a quartered raw onion. The onion is very juicy and releases its juices quickly, at the same time that it adds flavor to the vegetables steaming with it.

Do not overcook your vegetables. If you steam your vegetables just long enough to take the starch out of them without their becoming limp, they will preserve their natural color and they will taste much better—and they will be more nutritious.

6. Chew your food thoroughly. Never eat hurriedly or under nervous strain or an emotional upset. All these things inhibit the normal functioning of your digestive system. Your body is the most wonderful, intricate mechanism on earth and, like any other good mechanism, can take a lot of wear and tear before it breaks down and needs repairs. We only hasten that day when we eat improperly of improper foods.

With these few principles in mind, you are now ready to start planning your own meals with a special emphasis on raw juice prophylaxis or therapy as the case may be. As a starter for you, I've prepared a few basic menus. These menus have been designed for a person in good health who wishes to attain optimum health. By comparing these foods in these menus with those given in the food chart on page 57 you can substitute foods of equivalent value and thus vary your menu from week to week.

The person who is suffering from some chronic ailment should first determine what nutrient or nutrients he is deficient in (the charts on pages 37 to 56 will help him do this). Then he should supplement these basic menus with the raw juices which will help him overcome this deficiency. He may also supplement his diet with those juice combinations which have been recommended for his specific ailment. (These have been listed alphabetically in chapter 6 of this book.)

MENUS

Everyday on arising: A freshly squeezed glass of the citrus bioflavonoids such as orange juice, grapefruit juice or diluted lemon juice. (Include some of the pulp.)

Everyday at mid-morning: A potassium broth cocktail (See
page 64.)

Menu No. 1

Breakfast:

Prunes in yogurt sprinkled with nuts

Lunch:

Large raw salad of tomatoes, lettuce, cucumbers,
onions and peppers.

(For a dressing that will give a tang to any salad, sprinkle
the salad with oregano and a little salt; then, crush a pod
of garlic in lemon juice and sprinkle it over the salad. This
will not only improve the taste of the salad, it will help
improve your health.)

Baked sweet potato.

Buttermilk.

Melon with cottage cheese, flavored with lemon juice.

A slice of whole grain bread of any kind.

Mid-afternoon: Carrot and Apple juice cocktail. (The
chronically ill person should substitute here a juice
recommended for his specific ailment.)

Dinner:

Small raw salad of lettuce and tomatoes.

Steamed carrots. (You may add just half a pat of butter if you wish.)

Steamed spinach, cooked with a small pod of finely
chopped garlic.

Broiled, lean, thinly sliced round steak with broiled
onions.

Tomato juice cocktail. (The chronically ill person
may here substitute his own specific juice cocktail.)

Just before retiring: A carrot and celery juice cocktail.

Menu No. 2

Breakfast:

Melon.

One soft boiled egg.

Buttermilk.

Whole grain bread of any kind. (One slice)

Lunch:

A raw salad of shredded cabbage, shredded carrots, chopped peppers, mixed with the salad dressing described previously and stuffed in half an avocado.

Carrot, beet and cucumber juice cocktail.

Soaked dried figs, chopped and mixed with honey and nuts in sour cream.

Dinner:

Small raw salad of lettuce and tomatoes.

Steamed chicken, made deliciously in the following manner: Grind some garlic with a little bit of salt and some oregano in a mortar. Rub this mixture on a small, lean chicken. Put a tiny bit of pure olive oil at the bottom of the pan so that the chicken won't stick to it. Smother chicken with onions, peppers and mushrooms. Add two very ripe tomatoes. Sprinkle with a pinch of basil, oregano and two bay leaves and let steam over a low flame until tender.

Steamed wild rice. (If you add a grated onion to it before steaming it will make it very savoury.)

Apple and carrot juice cocktail.

Crushed, fresh strawberries over a whole bran muffin. (You may top this, if you wish, with whipped cream cheese but be sure you buy the kind that is fresh and has not had a stabilizer added to it.)

Before retiring: Carrot and celery juice with a small part of parsley juice.

Menu No. 3

Breakfast:

Pear.

Muesli. (This is prepared by soaking a tablespoonful of oats in two to three tablespoonfuls of water overnight. The following morning add a grated raw apple—or the same quantity of prunes or mixed fruit—two tablespoonfuls of milk, a few drops of lemon or orange juice and a teaspoon of almond cream. You will find it quite a difference from the insipid processed cereals.)

Lunch:

Half a grapefruit.

A raw mixed salad of romaine lettuce, scallions (use the greens, too), watercress, tomatoes with a little bit of raw, shredded cauliflour stalk for a tang. Add half a cupful of seedless grapes and diced peaches for a surprise.

Baked potato.

Buttermilk.

Baked banana.

Mid-afternoon: Tomato juice.

Dinner:

A small raw lettuce and tomatoes salad.

Beets in sour cream.

Steamed Peas.

Broiled trout (or any other white, lean fish) sprinkled with crushed garlic, oregano, lemon juice and half a pat of butter.

Carrot juice.

Baked apple.

Before retiring: Carrot, celery and cucumber juice cocktail.

Menu No. 4

Breakfast:

Soaked dried figs and apricots.

Whole grain cereal sprinkled with raisins and nuts and covered with buttermilk.

Lunch:

Orange and grapefruit sections on lettuce with cottage cheese.

Tomato stuffed with grated cabbage, carrots, green peppers, onions and diced avocado.

Baked potato.

Carrot and cabbage juice.

Yogurt with fresh, sliced peaches.

Bran muffin.

Mid-afternoon: Apple and orange juice cocktail.

Dinner:

Small raw salad of lettuce and tomatoes.

Mushroom and onion omelette sprinkled with parsley.

Steamed cabbage creole. (Cut cabbage into approximately 1½ inch pieces. Add a quartered raw onion and a chopped green pepper. If you wish, you can include some mushrooms. Pour half a small can of tomato sauce or two very ripe tomatoes over this. Sprinkle with a tablespoonful of capers, a pinch of salt and a bay leaf and steam over a low flame until the cabbage is tender.)

Steamed turnips, mashed and mixed in with half a pat of butter and some finely chopped parsley.

Buttermilk.

Dried fruit compote sweetened with honey.

Before retiring: Carrot and celery juice.

Conclusion

All authors when, at last, they write "The End" to their book, do so with a sense of satisfaction for a work finished. But, at the same time, there is always that niggling feeling gnawing away on the edges of their intellectual conscience. Have I really said all I wanted to say? Have I given it the proper emphasis—the proper perspective? Have I been able to make my thoughts clear to you, my readers? Most of all, have I accomplished all I set out to do?

The debt of the author is double: he owes a debt to himself—and for that he writes the book; he owes a debt to his readers for, in offering his book, he is saying *Look here. I have something for you that will help you by making you happier or wiser or more understanding of people.*

I have paid the debt to myself: I had a book to write—and I wrote it.

But, have I paid my debt to you? I hope so—I've tried. I've tried to make you healthier and so happier and wiser. I console myself with the thought that in future editions I may perhaps succeed where now I've failed. I'll have succeeded if I've so convinced you of the value of raw juice therapy that you will try it. I'll count myself very successful if you keep coming back to this little book much like a good housewife keeps referring to her favorite cookbook 'til she has it memorized.

But the reader also has a debt to pay. His debt is to read —without prejudice, with honesty—what the author has to say and then *put it to the test*. Have you?

If we both have succeeded in paying our debts, this world of ours will be that much healthier, that much happier.

The End

Appendix, Index and Glossary

COMMON INHALANT, INGESTANT, AND CONTACT ALLERGENS

Feathers and animal dander are considered to be important causes of allergic rhinitis and asthma. Dander from cats, dogs, horses, cows, rabbits and guinea pigs, as well as feathers from chickens, geese, ducks, pigeons, parrots and canary birds are the most common.

Furs made from rabbits, skunk, beaver, mole, mink, goat or muskrat are important causes of hay fever in furriers and trappers, although a dermatitis may result from the dyes used in contact with the skin. Less expensive furs are usually altered and sold under different names. Feinberg lists the more important furs that are sold under different names.

Species	*Sold As*
Hare, dyed	Sable or fox
Hare, White	Fox
Rabbit, white	Ermine
Rabbit, white, dyed	Chinchilla
Rabbit, dyed	Sable
Rabbit, sheared and dyed	Seal, electric seal, Hudson Bay seal, muskrat
Muskrat, dyed	Mink, sable
Muskrat, pulled and dyed	Seal, Hudson Bay seal, Electric seal, Red River seal
Mink, dyed	Sable
Marmot (woodchuck)	Mink, sable, skunk
Opossum	Beaver
Goat	Bear, leopard
Fitch, dyed	Sable
Kid, dyed	Lamb
Otter	Sable
Nutria	Seal, beaver, otter

Horse dander and hair: Frequently used for pillows, covers, blankets, furniture, stuffing, automobile seats, carpet pads, cushions, mattresses, lining and padding clothes, sacks and bags, wigs, gloves, hats and furs.

Goat hair: Mohair covers, tapestries, plus covering in upholstered furniture, suits, linings, gloves, socks, felt hats, doll's hair, wigs, monkey fur, brushes and bedding.

Cat hair: Carriage robes, lynx and civet furs, slippers, toys and cheaper furs:

Dog hair: Rugs, Chinese rugs, cheaper furs and robes.

Rabbit hair: Dyed furs, felt hats, lapin fur, fur-lined gloves, angora wool in sweaters, collars, cuffs, scarfs, dresses and toys. Often advertised as "sable," "seal," "chinchilla," "fox," "hubian seal," "electric seal" or "Hudson seal."

Feathers: Chicken, turkey, goose, duck, pigeon, parrot, canary and feathers of other household birds or pets are found in pillows, furniture, feather beds, hats, dress trimmings, fans and dusters.

Sheep wool: May cause symptoms when in the raw state as in blankets, robes, mattresses or furniture and wool used for medical purposes. In the finished state as in clothing, hats, carpets or underwear it is seldom important as a cause of symptoms.

Camel hair: Jaeger wool, sweaters, portieres, shawls, alpaca, carriage robes, muffs, coats, trimming for coats, blankets, dress goods, hats, brushes, rugs, upholstered furniture and seats in cars.

Badger hair: Shaving brushes, floor brushes.

Hog hair: Mattresses, brushes, furniture, stiff brushes and toys.

Cattle hair: Carpet yarns, padding under carpets and rugs, blankets, Chinese rugs, mattress and furniture stuffing, felt, children's toys and doll wigs.

Ozite: This is a product of animal hairs, used as a padding under carpeting and rugs.

Cottonseed: Symptoms may be produced as an inhalant, an ingestant or by direct contact. Linters, used in mattresses, wadding, impure cotton, cushions, comforters, upholstery, fleece-lined underwear, waterproofing material, artificial silk, robes, medical and surgical muslin, gingham, turkish and cotton towels and celluloid will cause the symptoms, as will inhalation of fertilizers used on lawns.

As an ingestant, cottonseed is used in fertilizers, flour (as in doughnuts, cakes and cookies), French fried potatoes, oleomargarine, Crisco, Spry, Wesson Oil, Cottolene, Snowdrift, packing sardines, setting olives, candles, linoleum, oil cloth, bookbinding, setting chocolate, soaps, mustard and emulsions and liniments for external use. For those who are allergic to cottonseed, it is best to avoid all canned fish, cheap or adulterated olive oils, salad oils, salad dressings (unless the ingredients are known or made at home), pop corn, french fried, potatoes, pie crusts (unless made with lard) cake mix and gin.

Karaya gum*: Used in cathartics, drugs, certain foods, wave sets, certain brands of gelatin and junket, candies such as gum drops, jelly beans, hand lotions, hair waving solutions, emulsified mineral oils and laxatives, diabetic foods as soy bean and almond wafers, denture adhesive powder, fillers for lemon pies and custards, ices, flavors, salad dressings and tooth pastes.

Silk: Broadcloth, brocade, Canton crepe, chiffon, crepe de Chine, duchess satin, foulard, faille, georgette, taffeta, jersey, plush, pongee, rugs (oriental), poplin, radium, silk, wash satin, tub silk, tulle, thread, upholstery, tapestries, velvets, silk floss, for pillows, hosiery, lining, linit good, mufflers.

The following substances contain no silk, although their names would suggest some silk content: Kopak sunfast silk, rubberized rain-

---

*See Figley, K. D.: *Indian Gum (Karaya Gum) Sensitivity.* International Correspondence Club of Allergy, 7, 1937.

coats, Klostersilk, Silkatren, Rayon, Maxwell silk poplin, Esskay, unequaled best silk, subsilk, Japsilk.

Flax: Linen, flaxseed and linseed oil obtained from flaxseed poultices. "Uncle Sam's breakfast" also contains flaxseed and may produce allergic symptoms. Flaxseed is used as a meal seed for poultry. Linseed is pr~ent in linoleum, oil silk, patent leather, printer's ink, paint, varnishes and furniture polish.

Kapok: Pillows, mattresses, life belts, upholstered furniture.

Glue: There are two kinds of glue—animal and fish. Animal glue is obtained from the hides of horses, cows, sheep, hogs and rabbits, and from the bones and cartilages of sheep, calves, dogs, cats, goats, cattle and horses. Fish glue is made entirely from fishes.

Glue is used in cabinet making, bookbinding, capsules, mucilage and paint. Where furniture is old, dry and loose, dry glue may be a factor in causing asthma. Allergic symptoms caused by an allergy to glue are most ofter due to fish glue.

Tobacco: Tobacco smoke or the tobacco itself may be the cause.

Castor bean: Castor bean dust.

Orris root: scented face powder, body powders, bath salts, soap, tooth powder, soap powder, cleansing creams, etc.

Pyrethum: Insect powders or sprays, moth powders, incense, etc.

Derris Root: Active principle is rotenone used as insecticide and in flea powders.

POLLINATION SCHEDULE*

New England, eastern and central states: Maine, New Hampshire, Vermont, Connecticut, Rhode Island, Massachusetts, New York, New Jersey, Pennsylvania, Maryland, Washington, D.C., Virginia, West Virginia, Kentucky, Ohio, Indiana, Illinois, Michigan, and Wisconsin.

Trees:	Beech	April-May
	Birch	April-May
	Hickory	April-May
	Black walnut	March-May
	Cottonwood	April-May
	White ash	April-May
Amaranth group:	Spiny amaranth	June-September
	Pigweed (red root)	July-September
Grasses:	Sweet vernal grass	May-June
	Orchard grass	May-June
	June grass (blue grass)	May-July
	Timothy	June-July
	Red top	June-July
Plantains:	Plantain	May-September
Ragweed group:	Ragweed - short	August-October
	Ragweed - giant	August-October
	Cocklebur	July-September
Chenopod group:	Lamb's quarters	June-September
	Russian thistle	June-September
Dock group:	Yellow dock	May-July
	Sheep sorrel	May-July

Middle western states: Minnesota, Iowa, Missouri, Kansas, Nebraska, South Dakota, North Dakota.

Trees:	Black walnut	March-May
	Cottonwood	March-May
	Oak	April-May
	Hickory	April-May
	Beech	April-May
	Birch	April-May
	Summer cypress	July-October
Amaranth group:	Spiny amaranth	June-September
	Prostrate pigweed	June-September
	Red Root pigweed	June-September
	Western water hemp	July-October
Grasses:	Sweet vernal grass	April-July
	Orchard grass	April-August
	June grass	May-September
	Timothy	June-August
	Red top	June-September
Plantains:	Plantain	May-September
Ragweed group:	Ragweed - short	August-October
	Ragweed - giant	August-October
	Western ragweed	August-October
	Marsh elder	August-October
	Cocklebur	July-September
Chenopod group:	Lamb's quarters	June-September
	Russian thistle	July-September
	Annual salt bush	July-September
Wormwood group:	Sage brush	July-September
	Green sage	July-October
	Pasture sage	July-October
Dock group:	Sheep sorrel	May-July
	Yellow dock	May-July

Southern states: Georgia, Florida, Alabama, Tennessee, Mississippi, Arkansas, Louisiana, Oklahoma, Texas.

Trees:	Mountain cedar	December-February
	Cottonwood	February-April
	Black walnut	March-May
	Oak	April-May
	Pecan	April-May
Amaranth group:	Spiny amaranth	June-September
	Pigweed (red root)	July-September
Grasses:	Sweet vernal grass	April-July
	Orchard grass	April-August
	Perennial rye grass	May-July
	June grass (blue grass)	May-September
	Bermuda grass	May-September
	Timothy	June-September
	Red top	June-September
	Johnson grass	June-October
Plantains:	Plantain	May-September
Ragweed group:	Ragweed - short	August-October
	Ragweed - giant	August-October
	Cocklebur	July-September
	Marsh elder	August-October
Chenopod group:	Lamb's quarters	June-September
Dock group:	Sheep sorrel	May-July
	Yellow-dock	May-July

Southwestern states: Texas, New Mexico, California (southern portion).

Trees:	Mountain cedar	December-February
	Cottonwood	February-April
	Arizona ash	March-May
	Shad scale	March-June
	Oak	April-May
	Hickory	April-May
	Summer cypress	July-October
	Mesquite	May-August
Amaranth group:	Prostrate pigweed	June-September
	Red Root pigweed	July-September
	Careless weed	July-October
Grasses:	June grass	May-September
	Bermuda grass	May-September
	Johnson grass	June-October
Plantains:	Plantain	May-September
Ragweed group:	Slender ragweed	September-October
	Southern ragweed	September-October
	Rabbit brush	April-May
Chenopod group:	Lamb's quarters	June-September
	Russian thistle	July-September
Wormwood group:	Sage brush	July-September
Dock group:	Sheep sorrel	May-July
	Yellow dock	May-July

*This schedule gives only an approximate idea as to the various pollens found in the United States. Some of these pollens are more frequently hay fever offenders than others. In some districts the list may be larger than that presented. In California, where the pollen is abundant and the number of different pollens is great, the clinical problems become quite complicated. The information contained in the schedule was obtained from surveys conducted in various parts of the country to determine the local pollen flora.

POLLINATION SCHEDULE

Rocky Mountain states: **Montana, Idaho, Wyoming, Colorado, Utah.**

Trees:	Black walnut	March-May
	Cottonwood	March-May
	Shad scale	March-June
	Oak	April-May
	Hickory	April-May
	Beech	April-May
	Birch	April-May
	Summer cypress	July-October
Amaranth group:	Red root pigweed	July-September
	Prostrate pigweed	June-September
Grasses:	Sweet vernal grass	April-July
	Orchard grass	April-August
	June grass	May-September
	Timothy	June-August
Plantains:	Plantain	May-September
Ragweed group:	Western ragweed	August-October
	Cocklebur	July-September
	Ragweed - short	August-October
	Ragweed - giant	August-October
	Slender ragweed	September-October
	Rabbit brush	April-May
Chenopod group:	Lamb's quarters	June-September
	Russian thistle	July-September
	Annual salt bush	July-September
	Sage brush	July-September
Wormwood group:	Mugwort	July-October
	Green sage	July-October
	Pasture sage	July-October
Dock group:	Sheep sorrel	May-July
	Yellow dock	May-July

Pacific states: **Washington, Oregon, Nevada, California (northern).**

Trees:	Cottonwood	April-May
	Black walnut	March-May
	Shad scale	March-June
	Oak	March-June
	Olive	April-May
Amaranth group:	Red root pigweed	July-September
	Annual salt bush	July-September
Grasses:	Sweet vernal grass	April-July
	Orchard grass	April-August
	Perennial rye grass	May-July
Grasses:	June grass	May-September
	Bermuda grass	May-September
	Timothy	June-August
	Red top	June-September
	Johnson grass	June-October
Plantains:	Plantain	May-September
Ragweed group:	Cocklebur	July-September
	Western ragweed	August-October
	Slender ragweed	September-October
	Rabbit brush	April-May
Chenopod group:	Lamb's quarters	June-September
	Russian thistle	July-September
Wormwood group:	Sage brush	July-September
	Mugwort	July-October
Dock group:	Sheep sorrel	May-July
	Yellow dock	May-July

CALORIE TABLE

FOOD	MEASURES*	CALORIES
Almonds	12-15	100
Apple butter	1 tablespoon	40
Apples, baked	1 large and 2 tablespoons sugar	200
fresh	1 large	100
Applesauce, sweetened	½ cup	100
Apricots		
canned in syrup	3 large halves and 2 tablespoons juice	100
dried	10 halves	100
Asparagus, fresh or canned	5 stalks 5 inches long	15
Avocado	½ pear 4 inches long	265
Bacon	2-3 long slices cooked	100
Bacon fat	1 tablespoon	100
Banana	1 medium 6 inches long	100
Beans		
canned with pork	½ cup	150
dried	½ cup cooked	135
lima, fresh or canned	½ cup	100
snap, fresh or canned	½ cup	25
Beef		
corned	1 slice 4 inches by 1½ by 1	100
dried	2 thin slices 4 by 5 inches	50
hamburger steak	1 patty (4 to 5 per pound)	150
round, lean	1 medium slice (2 ounces)	100
sirloin, lean	1 average slice (3 ounces)	150
tongue	2 slices 3 inches by 2 by ⅛	50
Beet greens	½ cup cooked	30
Beets, fresh or canned	2 beets 2 inches in diameter	50
Biscuits, baking powder	2 small	100
Blackberries, fresh	1 cup	100
Blueberries, fresh	1 cup	90
Bologna	1 slice 2 inches by ½ thick	100
Breads		
Boston brown	1 slice 3 inches in diameter, ¾ thick	90
corn (1 egg)	1 2-inch square	120
cracked wheat	1 slice average	80
dark rye	1 slice ½ inch thick	70
light rye	1 slice ½ inch thick	75
white, enriched	1 slice average	75
white enriched	1 slice thin	55
whole wheat, 60%	1 slice average	70
whole wheat, 100%	1 slice average	75
Broccoli	3 stalks 5½ inches long	100
Brownies	1 piece 2 inches by 2 by ¾	140
Brussel sprouts	6 sprouts ½ inch in diameter	50
Butter	1 tablespoon	95

*1 cup equals 8 ounces. 3 teaspoons equal 1 tablespoon. 4 tablespoons equal ¼ cup.

135

FOOD	MEASURES	CALORIES

Cabbage, cooked ......½ cup 40
  raw ....1 cup 25
Cake
  angel ....1/10 of a large cake 155
  chocolate or vanilla,
    no icing ....1 piece 2 inches by 2 by 1 100
  Chocolate or vanilla,
    with icing ....1 piece 2 inches by 1½ by 1 100
  cup cake with
    chocolate icing ...1 medium 250
Cantaloupe .... ½ of a 5½-inch melon 50
Carrots ....1 carrot 4 inches long 25
Cashew nuts 4-5 100
Cauliflower ....¼ of a head 4½ inches in diameter.. 25
Caviar ....1 tablespoon 25
Celery ....2 stalks 15
Cheese
  American cheddar ..1 cube 1⅛ inches square
                  or three tablespoons grated 110
  cottage ....5 tablespoons 100
  cream ....2 tablespoons 100
Cherries, sweet ......15 large 75
Chicken
  broiled ....½ medium broiler 100
  roast ....1 slice 4 inches by 2½ by ¼ 100
Chinese cabbage ......1 cup raw 20
Chocolate
  almond bar ....1 bar 5-cent size 200
  fudge ....1 piece 1 inch square
              by ¾ thick 100
  malted ....fountain size 460
  mints ....1 mint 1½ inches in diameter 100
  plain bar ....1 bar 5-cent size 240
  sirup ....¼ cup 195
  unsweetened ....1 square 162
Cider, sweet ....1 cup 114
Clams ....6 round 100
Cocoa, half milk,
  half water ....1 cup 150
Cocoanut ....3 tablespoons dry 100
Cod liver oil ....1 tablespoon 100
Cod steak ....1 piece 3½ inches by 2 by 1 100
Cola soft drinks ......6-ounce bottle 75
Collards ....½ cup cooked 50
Cooking fats,
  vegetable ....1 tablespoon 100
Corn ....½ cup 50
Corn sirup ....1 tablespoon 75
Cornflakes ....1 cup 80
Cornmeal ....1 tablespoon uncooked 35
Cornstarch pudding ..½ cup 200
Crackers
  graham ....1 square 40
  peanut butter-cheese
    sandwich ....1 cracker 45
  round snack-type ..1 cracker 2 inches in diameter ... 15
  rye wafers ....1 wafer 25

FOOD	MEASURES	CALORIES
saltines	1 cracker 2 inches square	15
Cranberry sauce	¼ cup	100
Cream		
light	2 tablespoons	65
heavy	2 tablespoons	120
whipped	3 tablespoons	100
Cream-puff shells	1 shell	85
Cucumber	½ medium	10
Custard, boiled or		
baked	½ cup	130
Dates	4	100
Egg	1 medium size	75
Eggplant	3 slices 4 inches in diameter ½-inch thick	50
Endive	average serving	10
Escarole	average serving	10
Figs, dried	3 small	100
Flour, white or		
whole grain	1 tablespoon unsifted	35
Frankfurter	1 sausage	100
Gelatin, fruit flavored		
dry	3-ounce package	330
ready to serve	½ cup	85
Ginger ale	1 cup	85
Gingerbread,		
hot water	2-inch square	270
Grapefruit juice,		
unsweetened	1 cup	100
Grape juice	½ cup	80
Grape nuts	¼ cup	100
Grapes		
American or Tokay	1 bunch—22 average	75
seedless	1 bunch—30 average	75
Griddle cakes	1 cake 4 inches in diameter	75
Halibut	1 piece 3 inches by 1⅜ by 1	100
Ham, lean	1 slice 4¼ inches by 4 by ½	265
Hard sauce	1 tablespoon	100
Hickory nuts	12-15	100
Hominy grits	¾ cup cooked	100
Honey	1 tablespoon	100
Ice cream	½ cup	200
Ice cream soda	fountain size	325
Jellies and jams	1 rounded tablespoon	100
Kale	½ cup	50
Lamb, roast	1 slice 3½ inches by 4½ by ⅛	100
Lard	1 tablespoon	100
Lemon juice	1 tablespoon	5

137

FOOD	MEASURES	CALORIES

Lettuce ....2 large leaves 5
Liver ....1 slice 3 inches by 3 by ½ 100
Liverwurst ....1 slice 3¼ inches by ½ thick 100
Lobster meat ....1 cup 150

Macaroni ....¾ cup cooked 100
Maple sirup ....1 tablespoon 70
Margarine ....1 tablespoon 100
Marshmallows 1 20
Milk
  buttermilk ....1 cup 85
  condensed ....1½ tablespoons 100
  evaporated ....½ cup (1 cup diluted) 160
  skim milk, dried ....2½ tablespoons 100
  skim milk, fresh ...1 cup 85
  whole milk ....1 cup 168
  yogurt, plain ......1 cup 160
Mints, cream ....½-inch cube 5
Molasses ....1 tablespoon 70
Muffins
  bran ....1 medium 90
  1-egg ....1 medium 130
Mushrooms ....10 large 10
Mustard greens .....½ cup cooked 31

Noodles ....¾ cup cooked 100

Oatmeal ....¾ cup cooked 100
Oil (corn, cottonseed,
  olive, and peanut)...1 tablespoon 100
Okra ....10-15 pods 50
Olives
  green ....6 medium .... 5(
  ripe ....4-5 medium .... 5()
Onions ....3-4 medium 100
Orange ....1 medium 80
  juice ....1 cup 125
Oysters ....5 medium 100

Parsnips ....1 parsnip 7 inches long 100
Peaches
  canned in sirup.....2 large halves and 3 tablespoons juice .100
  dried ....4 medium halves 100
  fresh ....1 medium 50
Peanut butter ....1 tablespoon 100
Peanuts 10 50
Pears
  canned in sirup ....3 halves and 3 tablespoons juice 100
  fresh ....1 medium 50
Peas
  canned ....½ cup 65
  fresh, shelled ....¾ cup 100
Pecans 6 100
Pepper, green ....1 medium 20
Pickles, cucumber

sour and dill	10 slices 2 inches in diameter	10
sweet	1 small	10
Pies	(sectors from 9-inch pies)	
apple	3-inch sector	200
lemon meringue	3-inch sector	300
mincemeat	3-inch sector	300
pumpkin	3-inch sector	250
Pineapple		
canned, unsweetened	1 slice ½ inch thick and 1 tablespoon juice	50
fresh	1 slice ¾ inch thick	50
juice, unsweetened	1 cup	135
Plums		
canned	2 medium and 1 tablespoon juice	50
fresh	2 medium	50
Popcorn	1½ cups popped	100
Popovers	1 popover	100
Pork chop, lean	1 medium	200
Potato chips	8-10 large	100
Potato salad with mayonnaise	½ cup	200
Potatoes		
mashed	½ cup	100
sweet	½ medium	100
white	1 medium	100
Prune juice	½ cup	100
Prunes, dried	4 medium	100
Pumpkin	½ cup	50
Radishes	5	10
Raisins	¼ cup	90
Raspberries, fresh	1 cup	90
Rhubarb, stewed and sweetened	½ cup	100
Rice	¾ cup cooked	100
Roll, Parker House	1 medium	100
Rutabagas	½ cup	30
Salad dressing		
boiled	1 tablespoon	25
French	1 tablespoon	90
mayonnaise	1 tablespoon	100
Salmon, canned	½ cup	100
Sardines, drained	5 fish 3 inches long	100
Sauerkraut	½ cup	15
Sherbet	½ cup	120
Soup, condensed	11-ounce can	
Bouillon		25
Mushroom		360
Noodle		290
Tomato		230
Vegetable		200
Spaghetti	¾ cup cooked	100
Spinach	½ cup cooked	20

FOOD	MEASURES	CALORIES
Squash		
summer	½ cup cooked	20
winter	½ cup cooked	50
Strawberries, fresh	1 cup	90
Sugar		
brown	1 tablespoon	35
granulated	1 tablespoon	50
powdered	1 tablespoon	40
Sweetbreads	1 pair medium-sized	240
Swiss chard	½ cup leaves and stems	30
Tangerines	1 medium	60
Tapioca, uncooked	1 tablespoon	50
Tomato juice	1 cup	60
Tomatoes, canned	½ cup	25
fresh	1 medium	30
Tuna fish, canned	¼ cup drained	100
Turkey, lean	1 slice 4 inches by 2½ by ¼	100
Turnip	1 turnip 1¾ inches in diameter	25
Turnip greens	½ cup cooked	30
Veal, roast	1 slice 3 inches by 3¾ by ½	120
Waffles	1 waffle 6 inches in diameter	250
Walnuts	8	100
Watermelon	1 slice 6 inches in diameter 1½ inches thick	190
Wheat		
flakes	¾ cup	100
germ	1 tablespoon	25
shredded	1 biscuit	100

Alcoholic Beverages

FOOD	MEASURES	CALORIES
Beer	8 ounces	120
Gin	1½ ounces	120
Rum	1½ ounces	150
Whiskey	1½ ounces	150
Wines		
champagne	4 ounces	120
port	1 ounce	53
sherry	1 ounce	38
table, red or white	4 ounces	89-95

Courtesy of Metropolitan Life Ins. Co.

HEIGHT-WEIGHT TABLES

Desirable Weights for Men and Women of Ages 25 and Over*

Weight in Pounds According to Frame (as Ordinarily Dressed)

MEN

HEIGHT (with shoes on) 1-inch heels Feet Inches	SMALL FRAME	MEDIUM FRAME	LARGE FRAME
5 2	116-125	124-133	131-142
5 3	119-128	127-136	133-144
5 4	122-132	130-140	137-149
5 5	126-136	134-144	141-153
5 6	129-139	137-147	145-157
5 7	133-143	141-151	149-162
5 8	136-147	145-156	153-166
5 9	140-151	149-160	157-170
5 10	144-155	153-164	161-175
5 11	148-159	157-168	165-180
6 0	152-164	161-173	169-185
6 1	157-169	166-178	174-190
6 2	163-175	171-184	179-196
6 3	169-180	176-189	184-202

WOMEN

HEIGHT (with shoes on) 2-inch heels Feet Inches	SMALL FRAME	MEDIUM FRAME	LARGE FRAME
4 11	104-111	110-118	117-127
5 0	105-113	112-120	119-129
5 1	107-115	114-122	121-131
5 2	110-118	117-125	124-135
5 3	113-121	120-128	127-138
5 4	116-125	124-132	131-142
5 5	119-128	127-135	133-145
5 6	123-132	130-140	139-150
5 7	126-136	134-144	142-154
5 8	129-139	137-147	145-158
5 9	133-143	141-151	149-162
5 10	136-147	145-155	152-166
5 11	139-150	149-158	155-169

For girls between 18 and 25, subtract 1 pound for each year under 25.

Courtesy Metropolitan Life Ins. Co.

*These tables are based on numerous Medico-Actuarial studies of hundreds of thousands of insured men and women.

HEIGHT-WEIGHT TABLES

Height, inches	5 Yrs.	6 Yrs.	7 Yrs.	8 Yrs.	9 Yrs.	10 Yrs.	11 Yrs.	12 Yrs.	13 Yrs.	14 Yrs.	15 Yrs.	16 Yrs.	17 Yrs.	18 Yrs.	19 Yrs.
38	34	34													
39	35	35													
40	36	36													
41	38	38	38												
42	39	39	39	39											
43	41	41	41	41											
44	44	44	44	44											
45	46	46	46	46	46										
46	47	48	48	48	48										
47	49	50	50	50	50	50									
48		52	53	53	53	53									
49		55	55	55	55	55	55								
50		57	58	58	58	58	58	58							
51			61	61	61	61	61	61							
52			63	64	64	64	64	64	64						
53			66	67	67	67	67	68	68						
54				70	70	70	70	71	71	72					
55				72	72	73	73	74	74	74					
56				75	76	77	77	77	78	78	80				
57					79	80	81	81	82	83	83				
58					83	84	84	85	85	86	87				
59						87	88	88	89	90	90	90			
60						91	92	92	93	94	95	96			
61							95	96	97	99	100	103	106		
62							100	101	102	103	104	107	111	116	
63							105	106	107	108	110	113	118	123	127
64								109	111	113	115	117	121	126	130
65								114	117	118	120	122	127	131	134
66									119	122	125	128	132	136	139
67									124	128	130	134	136	139	142
68										134	134	137	141	143	147
69										137	139	143	146	149	152
70										143	144	145	148	151	155
71										148	150	151	152	154	159
72											153	155	156	158	163
73												157	160	162	167
74												160	164	168	171

From Sunderman and Boerner: "Normal Values in Clinical Medicine"

HEIGHT-WEIGHT TABLES

GIRLS

Height, Inches	5 Yrs.	6 Yrs.	7 Yrs.	8 Yrs.	9 Yrs.	10 Yrs.	11 Yrs.	12 Yrs.	13 Yrs.	14 Yrs.	15 Yrs.	16 Yrs.	17 Yrs.	18 Yrs.
38	33	33												
39	34	34												
40	36	36	36											
41	37	37	37											
42	39	39	39											
43	41	41	41	41										
44	42	42	42	42										
45	45	45	45	45	45									
46	47	47	47	48	48									
47	49	50	50	50	50	50								
48		52	52	52	52	53	53							
49		54	54	55	55	56	56							
50		56	56	57	58	59	61	62						
51			59	60	61	61	63	65						
52			63	64	64	64	65	67						
53			66	67	67	68	68	69	71					
54				69	70	70	71	71	73					
55				72	74	74	74	75	77	78				
56					76	78	78	79	81	83				
57					80	82	82	82	84	88	92			
58						84	86	86	88	93	96	101		
59						87	90	90	92	96	100	103	104	
60						91	95	95	97	101	105	108	109	111
61							99	100	101	105	108	112	113	116
62							104	105	106	109	113	115	117	118
63								110	110	112	116	117	119	120
64								114	115	117	119	120	122	123
65								118	120	121	122	123	125	126
66									124	124	125	128	129	130
67									128	130	131	133	133	135
68									131	133	135	136	138	138
69										135	137	138	140	142
70										136	138	140	142	144
71										138	140	142	144	145
72														
73														
74														

Facts about the Principal Vitamins

	PRINCIPAL SOURCES	PROPERTIES	PHYSIOLOGIC EFFECTS
Vitamin A	Fish liver oils, liver, eggs, milk, butter, green leafy or yellow vegetables	Oil-soluble; susceptible to oxidation, especially at high temperatures; nontoxic in recommended doses	Promotes bony growth; essential to normal function of epithelial cells and visual purple
Vitamin B$_1$ (Thiamine)	Yeast; whole grains; meat, especially pork, liver; nuts, eggs, legumes, most vegetables	Stable to heat, unstable to alkali; nontoxic in recommended doses	Carbohydrate metabolism, nerve function; promotes growth
Vitamin B$_2$ (Riboflavin) Vitamin G	Milk and cheese, plus the sources of B$_1$	Slightly water-soluble; unstable to light and alkali; nontoxic in recommended doses	Promotes growth, general health; essential to cellular oxidation
Nicotinic Acid (Niacin)	Same sources as for both B$_1$ and B$_2$	Water-soluble; stable; intolerance produces flushing, burning, itching (rare with Niacinamide)	Essential for health, tissue respiration, growth, gastrointestinal function, and normal skin
Vitamin B$_6$	Yeast, liver, cereals, fish	Colorless crystals; heat and alkali stable; soluble in water and alcohol; nontoxic in recommended doses	Essential for metabolism of certain amino acids
Vitamin B$_{12}$	Liver, beef, pork, glandular meats, eggs, milk and milk products	Dark red crystals or crystalline powder; soluble in alcohol; nontoxic	Maturation of red cells; neurologic complications of pernicious anemia; may be a growth factor
Vitamin C (Ascorbic Acid)	Citrus fruits, potatoes, cabbage, tomatoes, green pepper	Water-soluble; stable in dry state but oxidized by heat and light; nontoxic in recommended doses	Essential to osteoid tissue, collagen formation, vascular function, and tissue respiration; essential in wound healing
Vitamin D D$_2$ (Calciferol) D$_3$ (Activated cholesterol)	Fish liver oils, eggs, milk, butter, sunlight and irradiation	Oil-soluble; in large doses may cause hypercalcemia	Metabolism of calcium and phosphorus
Folic Acid	Green leafy vegetables, liver and kidney	Crystalline powder; soluble in dilute aqueous alkali; nontoxic in recommended doses	Maturation of red blood cells; may be concerned in protein metabolism
Vitamin K (Activity)	Intestinal bacterial synthesis and a normal diet		Prothrombin formation; normal blood coagulation
Menadione		Oil soluble in water; unstable to light; nontoxic in recommended doses	
Menadione sodium bisulfite		Soluble in water; unstable with alkalis; nontoxic in recommended doses	
Vitamin K$_1$		Oily liquid; unstable to heat and light; insoluble in water	

Facts about the Principal Vitamins

DEFICIENCY SYMPTOMS	DAILY ALLOWANCES				THERAPEUTIC DOSAGE
Night blindness Xerophthalmia Hyperkerstosis of skin	Children under 1 1-3 4-6 7-9 10-12 Girls 13-20	units 1,500 2,000 2,500 3,500 4,500 5,000	Boys 13-15 16-20 Women Preg. Lact. Men	units 5,000 6,000 5,000 6,000 8,000 5,000		Up to 100,000 u./day
Beriberi Peripheral neuritis (Gastrointestinal disturbances)	Children under 1 1-3 4-6 7-9 10-12 Girls 13-15 16-20	mg. 0.4 0.6 0.8 1.0 1.2 1.4 1.2	Boys 13-15 16-20 Women Preg. Lact. Men	mg. 1.6 2.0 1.2-1.8 1.8 2.3 1.5-2.3		10-100 mg./day
Cheilosis Keratitis Glossitis Photophobia Follicular keratosis	Children under 1 1-3 4-6 7-9 10-12 Girls 13-15 16-20	mg. 0.6 0.9 1.2 1.5 1.8 2.0 1.8	Boys 13-15 16-20 Women Preg. Lact. Men	mg. 2.4 3.0 1.8-2.7 2.5 3.0 2.2-3.3		5-15 mg./day
Pellagra: (Dermatitis, glossitis, gastrointestinal disturbance, nervous system dysfunction)	Children under 1 1-3 4-6 7-9 10-12 Girls 13-15 16-20	mg. 4.0 6.0 8.0 10.0 12.0 14.0 16.0	Boys 13-15 16-20 Women Preg. Lact. Men	mg. 16.0 20.0 12.0-18.0 18.0 23.0 15.0-23.0		50-500 mg./day
Seborrhea-like skin lesions; epileptiform convulsions in infants; (vomiting of pregnancy)	1.5 to 2 mg. daily					50 to 100 mg. daily
Pernicious anemia;	Not established but is considered an essential nutrient					1 mcg. a day I. M. to retain remission in pernicious anemia
Scurvy: (Hemorrhages, loose teeth, gingivitis)	Children under 1 1-3 4-6 7-9 10-12 Girls 13-20	mg. 30.0 35.0 50.0 60.0 75.0 80.0	Boys 13-15 16-20 Women Preg. Lact. Men	mg. 90.0 100.0 70.0 100.0 150.0 75.0		100-1,000 mg./day
Infantile rickets Infantile tetany Osteomalacia	Infants Prematurity Children Pregnancy Lactation			units 800- 1,200 5,000-10,000 400 800 800		Up to 300,000 u./day
Nutritional macrocytic anemia	0.5 to 1 mg. daily					5 to 20 mg. every day
Hemorrhage from prolonged prothrombin time	Undetermined 2.5 mg. (or more) daily (with bile salts when indicated) 2.5 mg. (or more) daily (bile salts not necessary' 50-150 mg. IV for hemorrhage due to anticoagulant therapy					

National Research Council

RECOMMENDED DIETARY ALLOWANCES

	AGE YEARS	WEIGHT KG. (LB.)	HEIGHT CM. (IN.)	CALORIES
Men......	25	65 (143)	170 (67)	3200[2]
	45	65 (143)	170 (67)	2900
	65	65 (143)	170 (67)	2600
Women....	25	55 (121)	157 (62)	2300[2]
	45	55 (121)	157 (62)	2100
	65	55 (121)	157 (62)	1800
	Pregnant (3rd trimester)			Add 400
	Lactating (850 ml. daily)			Add 1000
Infants[3]	0–1/12[4]			
	1/12–3/12	6 (13)	60 (24)	kg.x120
	4/12–9/12	9 (20)	70 (28)	kg.x110
	10/12–1	10 (22)	75 (30)	kg.x100
Children.	1–3	12 (27)	87 (34)	1200
	4–6	18 (40)	109 (43)	1600
	7–9	27 (59)	129 (51)	2000
Boys	10–12	35 (78)	144 (57)	2500
	13–15	49 (108)	163 (64)	3200
	16–20	63 (139)	175 (69)	3800
Girls ...	10–12	36 (79)	144 (57)	2300
	13–15	49 (108)	160 (63)	2500
	16–20	54 (120)	162 (64)	2400

---

[1] In planning practical dietaries, the recommended allowances can be attained with a variety of common foods which will also provide other nutrient requirements less well known; the allowance levels are considered to cover individual variations among normal persons as they live in the United States subjected to ordinary environmental stresses.

National Research Council

RECOMMENDED DIETARY ALLOWANCES

PROTEIN GM.	CALCIUM GM.	IRON MG.	VITAMIN A I.U.	THIAMINE MG.
65	0.8	12	5000	1.6
65	0.8	12	5000	1.5
65	0.8	12	5000	1.3
55	0.8	12	5000	1.2
55	0.8	12	5000	1.1
55	0.8	12	5000	1.0
80	1.5	15	6000	1.5
100	2.0	15	8000	1.5
kg.x3.5[3]	0.6	6	1500	0.3
kg.x3.5[3]	0.8	6	1500	0.4
kg.x3.5[3]	1.0	6	1500	0.5
40	1.0	7	2000	0.6
50	1.0	8	2500	0.8
60	1.0	10	3500	1.0
70	1.2	12	4500	1.3
85	1.4	15	5000	1.6
100	1.4	15	5000	1.9
70	1.2	12	4500	1.2
80	1.3	15	5000	1.3
75	1.3	15	5000	1.2

[2] These calorie recommendations apply to the degree of activity for the average active man and woman. For the urban "white-collar" worker they are probably excessive. In any case, the calorie allowance must be adjusted to the actual needs of the individual as required to achieve and maintain his desirable weight.

[3] The recommendations for infants pertain to nutrients derived primarily from cow's milk. If the milk from which the protein is

National Research Council

RECOMMENDED DIETARY ALLOWANCES

	RIBO-FLAVIN MG.	NIACIN MG	ASCORBIC ACID MG.	VITAMIN D I.U
Men	1.6	16	75	
	1.6	15	75	
	1.6	13	75	
Women	1.4	12	70	
	1.4	11	70	
	1.4	10	70	
	2.0	15	100	400
	2.5	15	150	400
Infants[3]	0.4	3	30	400
	0.7	4	30	400
	0.9	5	30	400
Children	1 0	6	35	400
	1 2	8	50	400
	1.5	10	60	400
Boys	1 8	13	75	400
	2 1	16	90	400
	2 5	19	100	400
Girls.....	1 8	12	75	400
	2.0	13	80	400
	1.9	12	80	400

derived is human milk or has been treated to render it more digestible, the allowance may be in the range of 2-3 gms. per kg. There should be no question that human milk is a desirable source of nutrients for infants even though it may not provide the levels recommended for certain nutrients. (See discussion in text.)

[4] During the first month of life, desirable allowances for many nutrients are dependent upon maturation of excretory and endocrine functions. Therefore no specific recommendations are given.

OBSTETRIC TABLE The calculation is made from the first day of the last menstrual period.

Month	1	2	3	4	5	6	7	8	9	10	11	12	13	14	15	16	17	18	19	20	21	22	23	24	25	26	27	28	29	30	31	Month
January	1	2	3	4	5	6	7	8	9	10	11	12	13	14	15	16	17	18	19	20	21	22	23	24	25	26	27	28	29	30	31	January
October	8	9	10	11	12	13	14	15	16	17	18	19	20	21	22	23	24	25	26	27	28	29	30	31	1	2	3	4	5	6	7	*November*
February	1	2	3	4	5	6	7	8	9	10	11	12	13	14	15	16	17	18	19	20	21	22	23	24	25	26	27	28				February
November	8	9	10	11	12	13	14	15	16	17	18	19	20	21	22	23	24	25	26	27	28	29	30	1	2	3	4	5				*December*
March	1	2	3	4	5	6	7	8	9	10	11	12	13	14	15	16	17	18	19	20	21	22	23	24	25	26	27	28	29	30	31	March
December	6	7	8	9	10	11	12	13	14	15	16	17	18	19	20	21	22	23	24	25	26	27	28	29	30	31	1	2	3	4	5	*January*
April	1	2	3	4	5	6	7	8	9	10	11	12	13	14	15	16	17	18	19	20	21	22	23	24	25	26	27	28	29	30		April
January	6	7	8	9	10	11	12	13	14	15	16	17	18	19	20	21	22	23	24	25	26	27	28	29	30	31	1	2	3	4		*February*
May	1	2	3	4	5	6	7	8	9	10	11	12	13	14	15	16	17	18	19	20	21	22	23	24	25	26	27	28	29	30	31	May
February	5	6	7	8	9	10	11	12	13	14	15	16	17	18	19	20	21	22	23	24	25	26	27	28	1	2	3	4	5	6	7	*March*
June	1	2	3	4	5	6	7	8	9	10	11	12	13	14	15	16	17	18	19	20	21	22	23	24	25	26	27	28	29	30		June
March	8	9	10	11	12	13	14	15	16	17	18	19	20	21	22	23	24	25	26	27	28	29	30	31	1	2	3	4	5	6		*April*
July	1	2	3	4	5	6	7	8	9	10	11	12	13	14	15	16	17	18	19	20	21	22	23	24	25	26	27	28	29	30	31	July
April	7	8	9	10	11	12	13	14	15	16	17	18	19	20	21	22	23	24	25	26	27	28	29	30	1	2	3	4	5	6	7	*May*
August	1	2	3	4	5	6	7	8	9	10	11	12	13	14	15	16	17	18	19	20	21	22	23	24	25	26	27	28	29	30	31	August
May	8	9	10	11	12	13	14	15	16	17	18	19	20	21	22	23	24	25	26	27	28	29	30	31	1	2	3	4	5	6	7	*June*
September	1	2	3	4	5	6	7	8	9	10	11	12	13	14	15	16	17	18	19	20	21	22	23	24	25	26	27	28	29	30		September
June	8	9	10	11	12	13	14	15	16	17	18	19	20	21	22	23	24	25	26	27	28	29	30	1	2	3	4	5	6	7		*July*
October	1	2	3	4	5	6	7	8	9	10	11	12	13	14	15	16	17	18	19	20	21	22	23	24	25	26	27	28	29	30	31	October
July	8	9	10	11	12	13	14	15	16	17	18	19	20	21	22	23	24	25	26	27	28	29	30	31	1	2	3	4	5	6	7	*August*
November	1	2	3	4	5	6	7	8	9	10	11	12	13	14	15	16	17	18	19	20	21	22	23	24	25	26	27	28	29	30		November
August	8	9	10	11	12	13	14	15	16	17	18	19	20	21	22	23	24	25	26	27	28	29	30	31	1	2	3	4	5	6		*September*
December	1	2	3	4	5	6	7	8	9	10	11	12	13	14	15	16	17	18	19	20	21	22	23	24	25	26	27	28	29	30	31	December
September	7	8	9	10	11	12	13	14	15	16	17	18	19	20	21	22	23	24	25	26	27	28	29	30	1	2	3	4	5	6	7	*October*

TEMPERATURE and PULSE

TEMPERATURE OF THE BODY

The average normal temperature of adults is 98.6° F.; of the aged, 98.8°; of children, 99°.

The daily variation is from 1° to 1.5°, the maximum temperature being reached between 5 and 7 p. m.

RELATION OF PULSE AND TEMPERATURE

A variation of one degree of temperature, above 98° F., is approximately equivalent to a difference of ten beats in the pulse, thus:

Temperature of 98° F. corresponds with pulse of 60
Temperature of 99° F. corresponds with pulse of 70
Temperature of 100° F. corresponds with pulse of 80
Temperature of 101° F. corresponds with pulse of 90
Temperature of 102° F. corresponds with pulse of 100
Temperature of 103° F. corresponds with pulse of 110
Temperature of 104° F. corresponds with pulse of 120
Temperature of 105° F. corresponds with pulse of 130
Temperature of 106° F. corresponds with pulse of 140

THE PULSE, AVERAGE FREQUENCY AT
DIFFERENT AGES IN HEALTH

AGE	BEATS PER MINUTE (CARPENTER)	BY OTHER AUTHORITIES
In the fetus in utero..... ..between	150—140..	
Newborn infants......... ..between	140—130.	150—130
During first year........... .from	130—115.	130—108
During second year....... from	115—100.	108— 90
During third year.. ..... .from	105— 95...	90— 80
From 7th to 14th year. . .from	90— 80	80— 72
From 14th to 21st year. `.from	85— 75..	85— 80
From 21st to 60th year. ..from	75— 80	Av. 72
In old age ....between	75— 80	Av. 67

The pulse is generally more rapid in females, by 10—14 beats per minutes; during and after exertion unless long continued; during digestion or mental excitement, and generally more frequent in the morning. It is less rapid in the nervous as well as in those of phlegmatic temperament.

RESPIRATION and BLOOD PRESSURE

THE RESPIRATION AT VARIOUS AGES

Age	Number of Respirations per Minute
First year	25—35
At puberty	20—25
Adult age	16—18

AVERAGE NORMAL BLOOD PRESSURE

Age	Systolic	Diastolic	Pulse Pressure
10 years	103	70	33
15 years	113	75	38
20 years	120	80	40
25 years	122	81	40
30 years	123	82	41
35 years	124	83	41
40 years	126	84	42
45 years	128	85	43
50 years	130	86	44
55 years	132	87	45
60 years	135	89	46

NORMAL FINDINGS

URINE ANALYSIS

Volume in 24 hours	750-2,000 cc.
p.H.	4.8-7.5
Specific Gravity	1.015-1.020
Total Nitrogen	12-18 gm. in 24 hrs.
Urea Nitrogen	10-40 gm. in 24 hrs.
Creatinine	1,000-1,500 mgm. 24 hrs.
Ammonia Nitrogen	600 mgm. in 24 hrs.
Uric Acid	400-1,000 mgm. in 24 hrs.
Chloride (as Sodium Chloride)	10-15 gm. in 24 hrs.
Phosphates	1-2 gm. in 24 hrs.
Sulfates	1.5-3.5 gm. in 24 hrs.
Urobilinogen (Watson)	0-4.0 mgm.
Urinary Diastase (Amylase)	8-32 units
17 Ketosteroids	12-15 mgm. in 24 hrs.

KIDNEY FUNCTION

Phenosulfonephthalein test	+.75% excretion of dye in 2 hrs.
Urea clearance	75-130 per cent

BLOOD CHEMISTRY

Constituent	Test Material	mgm./100 cc.
Total solids	whole blood	19.23
Total protein	plasma	6.5-8.2
Albumin	plasma	3.8-6.7
Globulin	plasma	1.2-3.5
Fibrinogen	plasma	0.3-0.6
Total nitrogen	whole blood	3.0-3.7
Non-protein nitrogen	whole blood	25-35
Urea nitrogen	whole blood	10-15
Uric acid	whole blood	2.0-3.5
Creatinine	whole blood	1-2.
Creatine	whole blood	5-6
Amino acid nitrogen	whole blood	5-8
Ammonia nitrogen	whole blood	0.1-0.2
Undetermined nitrogen	whole blood	4-18

BLOOD CHEMISTRY (con't)

Constituent	Test Material	mgm./100 cc.
Hemoglobin		
(men)	whole blood	14-17 (gms. per 100 cc.)
(women)	whole blood	13-16 (gms. per 100 cc.)
Glucose	whole blood	80-120
Total Lipoids	plasma	450-550
Total Fatty Acids	plasma	190-450
Neutral Fat	plasma	0-370
Cholesterol	plasma	130-230
Lecithin (Phospholipids)	plasma	60-350
Bilirubin	serum	0.1-0.8
Chlorides (as Sodium Chloride)	whole blood	450-500
Chlorides (as Sodium Chloride)	plasma	570-620
Sulfates (inorganic as S)	whole blood	1.04±0.05
Phosphorus, inorganic	plasma	3.7-5.0
Calcium	serum	9.3-11.0
Magnesium	serum	1-3
Sodium	serum	330
	whole blood	310-345
Potassium	serum	16-22
Diastase (Amylase)	plasma or serum	80-150
Vitamin C (Ascorbic acid)	plasma	0.8-2.4
Iodine (Protein bound)	serum	3.5-8.5 gamma
Lipase	plasma or serum	Less than 1.5 cc. of N/20 Na OH
Alkaline Phosphatase—Adult	serum	1.5-4.0 Bodansky units
Children	serum	5-12 Bodansky units
CO_2 Combining Power	plasma	50-80 vol.per cent
Hydrogen ion conc.	whole blood serum	pH 7.4 pH 7.6-7.9

NORMAL FINDINGS

CEREBROSPINAL FLUID

Amount .... 60-150 cc.

Specific Gravity 1.001-1.010

Reaction .... alkaline

Total solids .... 0.8-1.2 gm./100 cc.

Calcium .... 2.5-11.2 mgm./100 cc.

Chlorides .... 740 mgm./100 cc.

Sugar .... 45-85 mgm./100 cc.

Total protein .... 15-40 mgm./100 cc.

GASTRIC CONTENTS

Volume .... 20-50 cc.

Free Hydrochloric acid
(Topfer's) .. 20-40 degrees (cc. N/10 Na OH per 100 cc.)

Total Acidity .. 40-70 degrees (cc. N/10 Na OH per 100 cc.)

DUODENAL CONTENTS

Pancreatic Amylase (Amylopsin) .... 40 units

Pancreatic Lipase
(Steapsin) 0.3-4.3 cc. of N/20 Na OH (Lipolytic Activity)

Trypsin .... 25-50 mm. (gelatin digested)

FECES

Dry solids .... 15-35 per cent

Total fats .... not to exceed 20 per cent

Urobilinogen .... 40-280 mgm. per day

LIVER FUNCTION TESTS

Normal Values

Serum Bilirubin—less than .... 1.0 mgm./100 of serum

Cephalin-cholesterol—less than .... .4 units
Flocculation (Hanger)

Urobilinogen in urine—less than .... 1.2 Ehrlich units
(Watson)

Bromsulphalein Excretion No retention of dye after 45 min.

Icterus Index (Bilirubin content) 4-6

Hippuric Acid Excretion
Oral test ... 3.0 gm. of Sodium Benzoate as Benzoic acid

Intravenous
test ... 0.7 gm. of Sodium Benzoate as Benzoic acid

Galactose Tolerance

Galactose Tolerance .. Less than 3.0 gms. of sugar excreted
in 5 hr. test period

Levulose Tolerance .... Blood sugar not to rise above
130 mgm./100 cc. of blood

Thymol Turbity .... 0-4 units

Cholesterol—
cholesterol ester ratio .... 60-69% of total cholesterol

Iso—Iodeikon Test .... 10% retention in serum ½ hr.
5% or less retention in serum 1 hr
(greater the retention, the greater the
impaired liver function)

HEMATOLOGY

Coagulation time (Lee-White) .... 5-8 minutes

Bleeding time .... 1-2 minutes

Contraction of clot .... 1-2 hours.

Prothrombin time (Quick) .... 22-25 seconds

Prothrombin time
(Shapiro)—whole blood .... 15.5 seconds ±1.5
diluted blood ..... 39.5 seconds ±2.5

Erthrocyte Sedimentation Rate
Westergren—men .... 1-5 mm./hr.
women .... 2-0 mm./hr.

Linsenmeier—men .... 350-600 minutes
women .... 300-600 minutes

Wintrobe—men .... 0-9 mm./hr.
women .... 0-20 mm./hr.

CARDIAC HEMODYNAMICS
(CARDIAC CATHETERIZATION)

Right auricular mean pressure .. . —2 to +3 mm. Hg

Right ventricular pressure .... .25 systolic
2 diastolic
mean 13

Pulmonary artery .... 25/8 mean 15

Brachial artery .... 120/70 mean 90

Cardiac index (cc/mm/m2) .... 3.1±0.4

A-V O₂ difference 4.2-4.7

Stroke volume—cc. .... .80

O₂ consumption (cc/min/m²) 150

Peripheral resistance (dynes/sec./cm⁻⁵) 1130-1216

HOW IMPORTANT
IS FOOD HEALTHWISE?

(In "Consumers Bulletin,,' September, 1957 issue, an article entitled "The Food You Eat" quotes from statements made by Dr. Tom Douglas Spies at the 1957 Annual Meeting of the American Medical Association as follows:)

"All diseases are caused by chemicals, and all diseases can be cured by chemicals. All chemicals used by the body--except for the oxygen which we breathe and the water which we drink--are taken in through food. <u>If we only knew enough, all diseases could be prevented, and could be cured, through proper nutrition...</u>

"As tissues become damaged, they lack the chemicals of good nutrition, they tend to become old. They lack what I call 'tissue integrity'. If we can help the tissues repair themselves by correcting nutritional deficiencies, we can make old age wait."

Acid Ash Residue—The inorganic substances, chieflly chloride, sulfate and phosphate, which form acid compounds in the body.

Acid-Base Balance—of body fluids, and tissues. A delicate balance exists between the two at all times, and is higher or lower in different parts of the body. A slight alkalinity of the blood is normal. Disease severely alters the alkalinity of the blood and probably of some of the body tissues.

Acidosis—A condition caused by the abnormal accumulation of acids in, or the excessive loss of base from the body.

Acid-Forming Foods—Foods in which the acid ash residue exceeds the alkaline ash residue: meat, fish, poultry, eggs, cereals and some nuts.

Alkaline Ash Residue—The elements sodium, potassium, calcium, and magnesium, which form alkaline compounds in the body.

Alkaline Forming Foods—Foods in which the alkaline ash residue exceeds the acid ash residue: most fruits, vegetables, and milk.

Amino Acids—Constituents of protein. Some 23 of them are known to be important to the body. Some are found in certain plants: lysine is plentiful in ripe peas, in green beans, in various kinds of cabbage. Tryptophan is found in the protein of soy bean, brussel sprouts and green cabbage and in the green leaves of cauliflower.

Allergy—Reaction to a specific substance which causes symptoms of hypersensitivity in those who are especially sensitive to it.

Base—Unites with an acid to form a salt. See Alkaline.

Cellulose—Form of carbohydrates which contributes little to actual nutrition, but must be in proper proportion in the diet for the mechanics of digestion and the hygiene of the digestive tract. Contributes bulk. Soft celluloses and hemicelluloses are in ordinary fruits and vegetables.

Cholesterol—A fat like substance found in animal tissues; may be synthesized in the body. It is excreted in the bile, but largely reabsorbed from the digestive tract in the presence of fat.

Congestion— Excessive amount of blood in a part of the body.

Enzyme—A substance formed by living cells, which have a specific action in promoting chemical changes and are essentially basic to life. Many work together in intricate interaction to bring about every step in the living process, for example, digestion of food, building of tissues. No enzyme has yet been synthesized by man in the laboratory.

Fruits—These are especially important because of their laxative and base-forming properties and for their vitamins, as well as for their pleasant flavor. All fruits supply some ascorbic acid.

Leafy Vegetables—Chief value is in their vitamin and mineral content. Leaves that are thin and contain the most chlorophyll are richest in vitamins. They are especially rich in Vitamin A, ranking next to milk in this. The leaf is a good source of calcium and phosphorus and is of great importance as a source of iron.

Metabolic—Referring to all chemical changes which occur to substances within the body after absorption. These changes include constructive and destructive processes.

Mineral—Inorganic elements. The following are known to be present in the body tissue: calcium, cobalt, chlorine, copper, fluorine, iodine, iron, magnesium, manganese, molybdenum, phosphorus, potassium, sodium, sulfur, zinc. Those obtained from food aid in the regulation of the acid-base balance of the body, and of osmotic pressure, in addition to their specific functions individually. Some are present in the body in organic combinations, for example, iron in hemoglobin.

Organic—Referring to the animal or vegetable kingdom as opposed to the mineral. Often used to mean "vital" as opposed to "physical."

Roughage—All material not dissolved by the digestive enzymes. Of value not only because of the vitamin carrying properties of the rough foods, such as vegetables, but also because it in the long run favors best functional activity of the large intestine and promotes proper evacuation. It is also thought that the "unavailable carbohydrate" of crude fiber may have a protein-sparing action.

Seed Vegetables, or Legumes—Chief among these are beans and peas. Their value lies chiefly in richness of protein. In their dry state they contain, pound for pound, an even greater amount of protein than meat. They are also rich in carbohydrate.

Supplement to the New Edition

Up until just recently one of the major barriers to the general acceptance of the idea that a relationship existed between elements in the soil and a person's health, was an almost universal belief among scientists that this was merely "an old wives' tale." I know of one case where a producer of an alfalfa nutritional supplement was sent to jail for claiming it to be so.

Now, it has become fashionable in some scientific circles to condescend to take a closer look at what Nature has been providing. It's known as the "Botanical Boom" among the salesmen attached to drug companies.

More specifically, for example, is the case of a British study being conducted to test the belief that resistance to disease may be influenced by *trace elements* in the soil entering the body in drinking water or in the cells of fruits and vegetables. Dr. Henry V. Warren cited locations where health has been impaired by trace element deficiencies in the soil.

What has all this to do with Raw Juice Therapy? Just this, it is the first budding of hope that the truth about the benefits to be obtained from live foods will no longer be denied. Information about the importance of getting your vitamins and minerals every day from fresh raw juices is long overdue.

Calcium

Take Calcium, for instance. Calcium is very unevenly distributed in the body with over 99% of it normally in the bones. In adults there may be a long-continued loss of calcium without the appearance of specific symptoms. Oh yes, there may be nervousness and tiredness but these vague symptoms are often accepted without discovering the real cause. Too often tranquillizer pills are used to conceal the symptoms. But your dentist's x-rays will tell you that you are deficient in calcium because they show a gradual receding of the jaw bone from around the roots of your teeth. He takes this for granted as a sign of aging. But you can slow down this process by getting your full share of calcium. How? Especially from the leafy green vegetables. Milk, naturally, is also rich in calcium but I'd prefer to get it from leafy green vegetables and avoid the butter fats in milk. The lack of calcium in the blood and soft tissues may be replaced by calcium withdrawn from the bones. I suspect that this is related to painful arthritis in the joints. But on this I have no proof and I look forward to the time when some clinical research is directed this way. We're slowly getting there.

Potassium

Even in connection with Cancer. When Dr. Max Gerson began treating cancer from a nutritional standpoint in 1950 he was in danger of being expelled from the American Medical Association for being "unorthodox." Today the answers that cancer researchers finally are getting are from their "chemical attack" upon this disease. Dr. Gerson called it "restoring the proper chemical balance of the cell."

Dr. Gerson noted that in every case of cancer the patient also showed a potassium deficiency in his body cells. His drastic juice therapy regimen was intended to rectify this condition as well as to restore the other nutritional building blocks required to rebuild normal cancer-resistant cells. Remember then that these are the potassium-rich vegetables, fruits, and berries that are yours for the juicing: watercress, turnip tops, tomatoes, spinach, and especially radishes (too strong to drink alone). Parsley is also akin to radishes in this respect. Then we can add endive, dandelion, kale and cucumbers. And there's even more—apples, cranberries and fresh red beets. Further, there's that famous old-world theory about the "Grape Cure." Grapes have a very high percentage of potassium. Could that be in any way related to the belief that cures have been obtained from rigorous "grape cures"?

Plants—Nature's Way to Nourish Higher Forms of Life

Plants are the processing "factories" which Nature uses to extract food elements from the sun and soil. The plants process these elements and convert them into a form that can be assimilated by both animals and man. We know that the human body simply can't assimilate the minerals such as calcium, potassium, iron, etc.—no matter how badly they are needed for your health, unless they are first processed through plant life.

Vegetables contain these elements in relatively large amounts: calcium, phosphorous and iron. They also contain in minute amounts (but enormously important amounts) other substances which are essential to the body. Ordinarily, fruits and vegetables are not so rich in calcium that they can be depended upon as a prime source for this nutrient. However, the juice form makes possible a much greater intake of this element. Leaf and stem vegetables are generally richer in calcium, but the root vegetables, carrots and turnips, oranges and strawberries also offer us an invaluable source of it.

It should be known, however, that the green leaves whose calcium is available, such as broccoli, collards, kale, loose-leaf lettuce, and turnip tops are important preferably to spinach and other members of the Goosefoot family, because these latter contain so much oxalic acid as to render their calcium of little if any use. This is an example of the genuine differences between food values within the vegetable food group.

The green vegetables are also extremely important as sources of iron. In addition, they provide favorable conditions for its absorption into the body from the digestive tract and for its use in building blood hemoglobin.

One of the best reasons for including fresh, raw vegetables in the diet is to insure a sufficient intake of vitamins. We should remember here Dr. A. Van Haller's words: "When we speak of vitamins we should not think of 'nutrients' nor, even less, of 'additives to nutrients'; rather we should think of vital life-organizing forces. Every vitamin has its own particular structure, a definite very punctiliously upheld organization of the atoms which go to make it up." Every change in this living organization either changes or destroys the vitamin. Thus the vitamin is most effective as it exists and interacts with other elements in its live food form. Vitamins are highly sensitive to proportion.

Also vitally important in the live food are the enzymes. In fact, they govern every step in the life process. They are specific chemical catalysts. (All those known are proteins.) The New York Times announced that a single living cell contains 100,000 enzymes to produce its 1,000 to 2,000 chemical reactions.

It was also announced in the *Times* that some of the activities which enzymes are responsible for are "digestion of food, building of tissue, replacement of used up blood cells, conversion of chemical energy into kinetic energy, which in turn is responsible for movement and muscular activity." Each enzyme, it is now believed has a single minute specific step to produce in each complicated process, and works in union and interaction with other enzymes. The enzymes, in fact, according to the *Times,* "carry out extraordinary biochemical feats of far greater complexity than any of the biochemical processes thus far devised by man."

Never has an enzyme been synthesized by man in the laboratory. They may be destroyed, however, by wear, tear, or poisoning.

It is now believed that in certain diseases, hereditary or caused by defects in body metabolism, the body's ability to produce a particular enzyme may be missing. Many diseases, including the anemias, blood disorders, and perhaps diabetes, are now thought to be due to the absence, or reduction in activity of one or more enzymes. This development may bring a new stress in the field of nutrition on the live, raw enzyme-containing foods. (Enzymes are destroyed by as much heat as it takes to cause discomfort to the hand.)

Below is a discussion of some basic food values and their functions in the body, with a list of the effects caused by their deficiency, and a list of the vegetables (and fruits) which contain each. This should illustrate the immense importance of raw vegetables and their juices.

Magnesium: Lack of this results in increased heart beat (tachycardia), dilated blood vessels, lowered blood pressure, nervous disturbances, impaired digestion, and growth. Tests prove a deficiency in it gives tendency toward hysteria, insanity. It is essential to bone structure, muscular activity, normal nerves.

It is found in abundance in: green vegetables (magnesium is part of the chlorophyll complex, the green coloring matter of plants), beans, dried peas.

Magnanese: Necessary for tissue respiration, normal growth and reproduction. Tests have shown it to be essential to sexual instinct and sexual functioning. It is found in: green leaves of vegetables, peas.

Potassium: Vital to the control of body fluids especially adrenalin, heart rhythm, muscle function. Experimental diets deficient in potassium caused degeneration, slowed rate of growth, digestive distress, constipation, nervousness, insomnia. Kidneys enlarge and bones become abnormal.

Raw vegetables, green leafy vegetables and their juices make the best source of potassium. Raw potato juice is an exceptionally good source.

Calcium: Necessary for teeth, bones, muscle functioning,

heart, nervous system, blood clotting. C. E. Burtis in *The Real American Tragedy* relates tenseness, and irritability to a deficiency of it.

It is found in: certain types of vegetables, such as mustard greens, turnip greens, and kale. It is not in spinach, beet greens, or Swiss chard due to their oxalic acid content.

Iron: Necessary for the continual replacement of red blood cells which are destroyed every day. Women and children have a greater need for it. Anemia, intense fatigue, weakness, undue stress, and heart pounding have been related to a deficiency in it. It is found in: green vegetables, peas, beans.

Zinc: A constituent of insulin, and of enzymes. It is related to the metabolism of carbohydrates and of proteins. Deficiency in it is related to faulty digestion and a lowered rate of growth. According to Burtis, also, "Perhaps significantly, it has been found that in diabetes the pancreas contains far less zinc than normal." It is found in: nearly all foods. Fresh greens, beans and peas are good sources.

Vitamin C: Essential to the structure of the body, to the health of blood vessels and tissues. It is needed constantly since it is not stored in the body. It is needed in increased amounts during time of infection as it gathers around the site of the wound. It has also been related to tissue health in case of allergies.

It is found in: citrus fruits, green peppers, fresh greens, parsley.

THE POWER OF PLANTS

"The strength of your body lies in the juices of plants", a strong statement. Especially when you learn that it was made by the author of the world's first book on medicinal plants 5600 years ago!

Chinese Emperor Shin-Nong 3700 B.C.

Condition	Recommended Plant Juice and Why
Aging Symptoms	Artichoke Juice (lowers the cholesterin level in the blood, promotes functional work of the liver)
	Garlic Juice (promotes blood circulation, eases arterio-sclerotic difficulties, regulates blood pressure)
	Hawthorn Juice (improves circulation, strengthens and supports metabolic action of the heart)
Allergies, Rashes, Pimples	Celery Juice (flushes out waste matter)
	Dandelion Juice (mobilizes waste)
	Stinging Nettle Juice (metabolic activator)
Anemia (caused by iron deficiency)	Spinach Juice (contains folic acid and iron, restores)
	Stinging Nettle Juice (contains iron, stimulates)
Appetite, loss of	Carrot Juice, for children (strengthens the stomach)
	Tomato Juice, for adults (promotes gastric juice of the pancreas)

Condition	Recommended Plant Juice and Why
	Wormwood Juice, for adults (increases gastric juice secretion)
Arterio-sclerosis	Garlic Juice (promotes blood circulation, eases arterio-sclerotic difficulties, regulates blood pressure)
	Hawthorn Juice (strengthens the heart, regulates blood circulation)
Arthritis	Birch-Leaf Juice (influences the cholesterol, promotes the elimination of uric acid from the blood)
	Celery Juice (dissolves and drains)
	Horse-Radish Juice, according to doctor's advice (promotes the blood circulation of the kidney)
Articular Difficulties	Birch-Leaf Juice, Horse-Radish Juice (eliminating and anti-inflammatory effect)

Condition	Recommended Plant Juice and Why
Asthma, Bronchial Breathing Difficulties	Coltsfoot Juice (loosens mucus) Onion Juice (for catarrhs of the upper air passage, mucus obstruction) Ribwort Juice (anti-inflammatory) St, John's Wort Juice (strengthens nerves — for functional breathing difficulties causéd by nervousness) Shave Grass Juice strengthens the tissue with its high silicic acid content) Thyme Juice (for spasmodic coughing fits)
Bile Deficiencies (functional)	Black Radish Juice (Essential oil — and magnesium — combination in black radish juice; stimulates the liver, promotes biliary flow) Dandelion Juice (stimulates bile formation in the liver) The two juices combined work to prevent formation of gall stones.

Condition	Recommended Plant Juice and Why
Bladder Catarrh	Birch-Leaf Juice (cleanses renal passages, has an anti-inflammatory effect) Shave Grass Juice (strengthens the tissues)
Blood Building, deficient	Hawthorn Juice (stimulates circulation) Yarrow Juice (relieves)
Blood Congestion	Hawthorn Juice (eases circulation) Yarrow Juice (promotes circulation, relieves, anti-spasmodic)
Blood Formation	Spinach Juice (high concentration of blood-forming vitamin "folic acid")
Blood Pressure (high)	Garlic Juice (lowers blood pressure Hawthorn Juice (strengthens the heart)
Blood Pressure (low)	Hawthorn Juice (normalizes blood pressure — the effectiveness explains itself from the improvement of the heart's work having a direct

Condition	Recommended Plant Juice and Why
	influence on the blood vessels) Yarrow Juice (stimulates blood circulation, anti-spasmodic)
Blood Renewal (Purification)	Celery Juice (stimulates the kidney, flushes waste matter out of the blood) Dandelion Juice (loosens waste matter, stimulates the liver and intestine) Stinging Nettle Juice (increases B.M.R. — basal metabolic rate)
Bronchial Catarrh	Coltsfoot Juice (loosens mucus, eases elimination) Onion Juice (loosens mucus) Ribwort Juice (anti-inflammatory) Shave Grass Juice (strengthens tissue & lungs through its silicic acid content)
Catarrh of the Respiratory Organ	See Breathing Difficulties under "Asthma"

Condition	Recommended Plant Juice and Why
Cholesterol Content of the Blood (too high)	Artichoke Juice (lowering effect) Birch-Leaf Juice (aids in eliminating uric acid)
Coldness, of the Extremeties	Hawthorn Juice (strenthens heart, stimulates blood supply, normalizes blood pressure) Spinach Juice (blood-building) Yarrow Juice (relieves tension and stimulates circulation)
Colds, flu-like	Red Beet Juice (increases power of resistance, improves normal breathing capability) Rose-Hip Drink mixed with Carrot Juice (raises natural immunity of the mucous membranes)
Cold, with a sore throat	Camomile Juice, Ribwort Juice (relieve pain and inflammation) Sage Juice for gargling (disinfects and cleanses)

Condition	Recommended Plant Juice and Why
Convalescent	Apricot Juice (strengthens and restores)
	Carrot Juice and Tomato Juice (rich in vitamins and minerals)
	Rose-Hip Drink (particularly rich in vitamins A and C)
Cough	Coltsfoot Juice (loosens mucus)
	Ribwort Juice (cleanses breathing passage, anti-inflammatory)
	Thyme Juice (anti-spasmodic, disinfects, cleanses)
Depletion, Exhaustion	Oat Meal (nitrogenous — restoring enzymes)
	Rose-Hip Drink (contains vitamins to increase resistance to infection)
Diarrhea	Silverweed Juice (constipates — through characteristic tannin —, soothes)
Diuretic Plant Juices	Celery Juice, Bean Juice, Cucumber Juice, Asparagus Juice (strong draining of the kidneys)

Condition	Recommended Plant Juice and Why
Dizziness	See Nervous Heart — and Circulatory Difficulties
Drainage, Diuretic	Celery Juice and Kidney Bean Juice (specific potash salts and essential oils of both juices work as a diuretic.
Dyspepsia	Sauerkraut Juice (regulates intestinal flora) Watercress Juice (eliminates) Wormwood Juice (strengthens and stimulates the stomach) Yarrow Juice (calms, eases cramps)
Female Difficulties	Borage Juice (powerful in the sense of a hormonal effect) Silverweed Juice (eases cramps Yarrow Juice (for nervous heartbeat, rapid pulse, dizziness or rush of blood to the head; equalizing effect on the vascular system, especially with menopausal difficulties)

Condition	Recommended Plant Juice and Why
Fever	Red Beet Juice (improves the power of resistance with its high vitamin content) Rose-Hip Drink (stimulates the power of resistance through vitamin C and Provitamin A)
Flatulence	Onion Juice (essential oils) Yarrow Juice (anti-spasmodic)
Gastric Catarrh	Silverweed Juice (relieves cramps) Wormwood Juice (regulates gastric activity) Yarrow Juice (soothes, anti-spasmodic)
Glandular Activity, excessive	Motherwort Juice, Valerian Juice (calming effect)
Glandular Activity insufficient	Parsley Juice, Watercress Juice (both stimulate due to specific enzymes) Stinging Nettle Juice (stimulates the metabolism)

Condition	Recommended Plant Juice and Why
Gums, Inflammation of the	Camomile Juice (anti-inflammatory, curative effect) Rose-Hip Drink (supplies vitamins) Sage Juice (through tannin and disinfecting oils, cleanses and strengthens)
Headache	Investigate the Cause! Hawthorn Juice (stimulates blood circulation) Parsley Juice (effective on the vascular system) Wormwood Juice (strengthens the stomach, effective for migraines due to the stomach)
Heartburn	Camomile Juice (eases cramps Potato Juice (for over-acidity of the stomach)
Heart Troubles (nervous)	Hawthorn Juice (increases blood flow to the heart, improves metabolic rate) Valerian Juice (induces sleep, day-time calming agent)

Condition	Recommended Plant Juice and Why
	Yarrow Juice (eases, dilates blood vessels)
Hoarseness	Ribwort Juice (cleanses, anti-inflammatory)
	Sage Juice, for gargling (disinfects)
Intestinal Cramps	Silverweed Juice or Wormwood Juice (anti-spasmodic)
	Yarrow Juice (relieves tension)
Intestinal Difficulties	Sauerkraut Juice (regulates — for disturbed intestinal flora following use of antibiotics or extended fasting)
	Wormwood Juice (stimulates peptic gland, strengthens the stomach-intestinal-muscle, promotes bile flow)
	Yarrow Juice and Camomile Juice (relieve cramps, calm, and are anti-inflammatory)

Condition	Recommended Plant Juice and Why
Intestinal Poisoning	Garlic Juice (normalizes intestinal flora, kills germs, cleanses the intestine) Sauerkraut Juice (regulates, normalizes the intestinal flow)
Kidney Stimulation	Birch-Leaf Juice (eliminates, anti-inflammatory) Celery Juice (eliminates) Shave Grass (strengthens the tissues)
Laxative	Apple and Sauerkraut Juice (normalizes the intestinal flora)
Liver Difficulties (functional type)	Artichoke Juice (strengthens the liver, stimulates cells, raises the capability to eliminate metabolic waste) Black Radish Juice (relieves bile duct, stimulates biliary flow) Dandelion Juice (stimulates the liver, promotes biliary flow)

Condition	Recommended Plant Juice and Why
	Watercress Juice (cleanses, eliminates)
Lumbago	See Rheumatism
Menopausal Difficulties	Borage Juice (stimulates a feeling of wellness)
	Silverweed Juice (balances)
	Valerian Juice (calms)
	Yarrow Juice (promotes circulation, eases, effective on the blood vessels)
Nerve Sedative	Valerian Juice (general sedative and stabilizer)
Nervous Debility	Oatmeal (strengthening)
	St. John's Wort Juice (restorative)
Nervousness	St. John's Wort Juice (strengthens, restores the nerves)
	Valerian Juice (calms the nervous system)
Rheumatism	Birch-Leaf and Cherry Juice (eliminates uric acid, anti-inflammatory)
	Juniper Berry Extract (cleanses, eliminates)

Condition	Recommended Plant Juice and Why
	Stinging Nettle Juice (metabolic activator)
Sciatica	See Rheumatism
Skin Blemishes (not infectious type)	Celery Juice (flushes out the impurities)
	Dandelion Juice (strengthens liver, cleanses blood)
	Parsley Juice (specific enzymes, potassium)
	Stinging Nettle Juice (stimulates metabolism)
	Watercress Juice (stimulates, blood-building)
Sleeplessness	Oatmeal (eliminating effect)
	Valerian Juice (nerve calming, sleep-inducing)
Slenderness	Celery Juice (eliminating effect)
	Stinging Nettle Juice (increases activity of all bodily organs)
	Watercress Juice (special glandular effect)
Spring Fever	See Blood Renewal, Purification

Condition	Recommended Plant Juice and Why
Stomach Acidity (excessive)	Potato Juice (soothes peptic gland, reduces gastric juice secretion)
Stomach Acidity (insufficient)	Wormwood Juice (regulates stomach activity, increases gastric juice secretion)
Stomach & Intestinal Cramps	Silverweed Juice (anti-spasmodic) Wormword Juice (strengthens the stomach) Carrot Juice (Provitamin A, phosphorous and calcium)
Vitamin Deficiency	Rose-Hip Drink (Vitamin complex carrier A,B,C,D,E)

Note: Herbal plant juices are more potent than fruit and vegetable juices. Several drops added to your usual combinations produce an intensified effect.

How do you obtain the herb juices?

1. Collecting fresh herbs in the wild and using your juicer.
2. Growing your own and using your juicer.
3. Buying fresh herbs at your natural health food store's produce section and using your juicer.
4. Buying bottled fresh-pressed herbal juices. Available at your health food store. Prepared by the Walter Schoenenberger family.
5. Steep herb tea for 10 minutes. Add 1 oz. to each 4 oz. of your raw juices to increase their effectiveness.

To increase your knowledge about herbs, see:

THE HERB BOOK

by John Lust (Bantam Books $3.95)

Available wherever books are sold.

14 day Raw Juice Diet
for a

SLIM FIGURE

The 14-day diet outlined has been tested and found to have excellent results in reducing weight while enjoying health-promoting meals. It is intended for normal healthy persons, who through thoughtlessness or overindulgence, have permitted excess weight to accumulate.

The menus are based on sound health principles. They are low in calories, adequate in protein, low in fats and carbohydrates and especially rich in vitamins and minerals. However, *should there be any physical condition existing which might be affected by a change in eating habits, we urge you to have a checkup by your physician, and have him prescribe your reducing diet.*

The diet is economical in that it requires no special foods which would not be acceptable to other members of the family. It is a normal diet, from which certain fattening foods have been omitted. You need only remove your portion of vegetables before butter is added for the others; or your meat before gravy is added; or your applesauce before sugar is added, and so on.

The main point of the diet, you will note, is to limit to the absolute minimum all fats, starches and sugars except those that are naturally in the foods permitted.

Follow this diet for two weeks. Do not eat anything not shown on the diet — and do not substitute anything if it can be avoided. But be sure to eat what is assigned for each day, rather than doing without. And bear in mind the following:

1. Vegetables should be prepared and served without butter. Use natural herbs such as oregano, basil, rosemary, parsley, chives, garlic, etc., to give them zest.

2. All sugar and cream should be omitted from beverages.

3. Salads should be served without mayonnaise or oil dressing.

4. Do not add sugar to grapefruit or other fruits.

5. Lean parts of meats, only.

6. Remember the success of the diet depends upon following it exactly.

7. Omit salt and other condiments, except the natural herbs.

Quantities should be moderate. Servings sufficient to satisfy hunger, without over-eating, and the menus should be followed closely.

Where this diet has been followed exactly, there has been a weight loss for the first two or three days of approximately two to four pounds. This is accounted for by the water being lost from the system. Then there might be a day or two when no change will be noted. After that the body will start to use up its stored fat and then the real loss in weight begins.

Keep up the diet for two weeks — no longer. After that, follow the maintenance diet. Some persons prefer not to watch the scale daily, and in many cases the psychological reaction is better with only a weekly weighing. For accuracy, the same scale — and the same amount of clothing — should be used. *Note carefully —and write down weight at beginning of the diet.*

The diet for the first seven days follows. After completing the first week, repeat the diet from the *first day* through the seventh.

When you have finished the 14-day diet it will be well to watch your weight so that any gain will be noted at once. As a matter of fact, one of the advantages of this diet is that you will become so aware of the benefits of the change in your eating habits that you will naturally follow a health-promoting maintenance diet as a natural and very enjoyable routine.

Fourteen-day reducing diet

Every morning — Immediately on arising, take an 8-ounce glass of warm water with the juice of 1/2 lemon. This acts as an internal bath, flushing the system of mucus and acids which have accumulated during the night.

This practice should be followed not only during the diet — but as a permanent, health-maintaining routine.

Breakfast: During the 14 days, breakfast every morning is the same and consists of the following:

Apple Juice — 8-ounce glass
Eggs — 1 boiled or poached (not fried)
Whole wheat toast — 1 slice — no butter substitute
Coffee black

Monday

Luncheon: Carrot Juice — 8-ounce glass

Broccoli, spinach or tomatoes

Eggs — 2 poached or hard boiled

Herb tea, with lemon if preferred, or health drink

Dinner: Carrot-Celery Juice — 8-ounce glass

Combination salad — lettuce, tomatoes, celery, cucumber — with lemon juice dressing if desired

Stoneground, whole wheat toast — no butter

Agar-orange jelly or stewed prunes

Herb tea, with lemon if preferred, or health drink

Evening: Carrot-Celery Juice (half and half) 8-ounces or plain celery juice

Tuesday

Luncheon: Carrot juice — 8-ounce glass

Salad — cottage cheese, pear, lettuce

Apple sauce — no sugar. Flavor with cinnamon if desired

Herb tea, with lemon if desired, or health drink

Dinner: Carrot-celery juice — 8-ounce glass

Steak, lean, broiled — medium portion

Salad — Tomato on lettuce — no dressing

Celery — 2 stalks

Baked apple — no sugar — stuffed with raisins

Herb tea, with lemon if desired, or health drink

Evening: Carrot-Celery juice — 8 ounce glass or plain celery juice

Wednesday

Luncheon: Carrot juice — 8-ounce glass
   Eggs — 2 poached
   Toast 1 slice stone ground whole wheat — no butter
   Stewed carrots and celery, or tomatoes
   Herb tea, with lemon if desired, or health drink
Dinner: Carrot-Celery juice — 8-ounce glass
   Lamb chops, 2 lean broiled
   Salad — celery, apple, cabbage, lettuce, grapefruit —
   no dressing
   Apple sauce — no sugar — flavored with cinnamon
   Herb tea, with lemon if desired, or health drink
Evening: Carrot-Celery juice — 8-ounce glass or plain
   celery juice

Thursday

Luncheon: Carrot juice — 8 ounce glass
   Cottage cheese on lettuce leaves
   Sliced oranges and thin sliced Bermuda onion
   Herb tea, with lemon if desired, or health drink
Dinner: Carrot-Celery juice — 8-ounce glass
   Liver broiled 2 small slices (not fried)
   Broccoli — no butter or sauce
   Agar jelly, orange or lemon flavor or 1/2 grapefruit
   Herb tea, with lemon if desired, or health drink
Evening: Carrot-Celery juice — 8-ounce glass or plain
   celery juice

Friday

Luncheon: Carrot juice — 8-ounce glass

Hot vegetable plate — broccoli, carrots, string beans, beets, celery

Herb tea, with lemon if desired, or health drink

1/2 grapefruit

Dinner: Carrot-Celery juice — 8-ounce glass

Filet of sole — broiled or baked *(not fried)*

Salad — apple, celery, orange, lettuce — no dressing

Stewed prunes or apricots

Herb tea, with lemon if desired, or health drink

Evening: Carrot-Celery juice — 8 ounce glass or plain celery juice

Saturday

Luncheon: Carrot juice — 8-ounce glass

Fruit salad — lettuce, chopped apple, celery, pineapple, cabbage — no dressing

Whole wheat crackers - 2

Herb tea, with lemon if desired, or health drink

Dinner: Carrot-Celery juice — 8-ounce glass

Broiled liver — 2 or 3 small slices (not fried)

Cooked vegetable — carrots, celery, string beans, green cabbage — no butter

Agar-orange jelly — or stewed prunes

Herb tea, with lemon if desired, or health drink

Evening: Carrot-Celery juice — 8-ounce glass

Sunday

Dinner: Carrot-Celery juice — 8-ounce glass

    Chicken roasted — no dressing — no gravy

    Cooked vegetable — broccoli, carrots, or string beans

    Salad — lettuce, chopped apples, celery, orange or grapefruit

    Prune whip

    Herb tea, with lemon if desired, or health drink

Supper: Carrot-Celery juice — 8-ounce glass

    Cold chicken 2 slices

    Fruit salad — no dressing

    Herb tea, with lemon if desired, or health drink

Evening: Carrot-Celery juice — 8-ounce glass

SPECIAL NOTES for the FOURTEEN DAY DIET

- Start your day with a glass of warm water with the juice of ½ lemon as soon as you get up.
- Breakfast every morning of diet is the same — apple juice, eggs, 1 slice whole wheat toast — no butter — and a herb tea or health beverage of some sort but without cream or sugar. Lemon if desired.
- Drink the apple juice as soon as extracted. Make a day's supply first thing in the morning. Take a glass — give some to other members of the family. Keep remainder in a tightly covered glass jar in the refrigerator.
- Eggs included in the specified menus should be boiled about four minutes, poached or hard boiled.
- If you must have coffee, drink it black at all times — or tea, with lemon if preferred. Use no sugar or cream. Caffeine-free.

- In selecting vegetables, be sure to select fresh, green or yellow vegetables. The greener the color, in spinach or broccoli for example, the richer is the vitamin content. When leaves start to turn yellow — or broccoli starts to blossom — it means the vitamins are being lost from the vegetables.
- In cooking vegetables, use very little water. Have it at the boiling point before putting in the vegetable. This prevents the oxidation of vitamins and minerals. Do not throw cooking water away. Drink it or use it for soups.
- Cook vegetables only until tender. *Do not overcook.*
- Select the large deep yellow carrots. The full-grown, orange colored carrots are richest in carotene or vitamin A.
- To prepare carrots for juicing — wash well in cold water, using a stiff vegetable brush. Scrape lightly, if necessary, but *do not peel.* Cut in convenient size pieces.
- Select firm juicy apples for juicing — they have more juice than the pulpy varieties. Wash in cold water — remove stem and bud ends. Do not core or peel, as valuable vitamins and minerals are in the core and skin.
- Do not add sugar to apple sauce, or baked apples. add a little cinnamon, if desired, for flavor.
- Select green lettuce — the outside green leaves have more vitamins and minerals than the white inside leaves.
- Select green celery with firm stalks. *Never use the leaves* of celery, as sprays frequently used by growers are injurious. For juicing, cut stalks in convenient size pieces, after thoroughly washing in cold water, and feed into the juicer.
- For the combination juices, make each one separately; that is, run the carrots through the juicer and then the celery. In this way you can be sure your proportions are correct in blending two juices.
- All vegetables should be washed thoroughly in cold water. Use several rinsing waters if necessary.
- Do not fry any kind of food. Meat and fish should be broiled, boiled or baked. If your range does not provide for broiling,

you can panbroil on the top of the stove by using an ungreased frying pan, and turning the meat frequently until it is cooked through. Or confine yourself to boiling or baking.

- If absolutely necessary, frozen vegetables may be substitutes for the fresh ones. Fresh is best, though.
- Serve foods as soon as cooked — or keep them tightly covered — to prevent oxidation of the nutrients.
- If you are hungry between meals, take a glass of apple juice or carrot juice at 10:30 a.m. and 4:00 p.m.
- Agar-agar, if available, provides bulk and encourages peristaltic activity necessary to overcoming constipation. Or else stewed mashed prunes may serve this purpose. Clear gelatine-flavored with fresh fruits and juices can be used for delicious, non-fattening desserts. The clear gelatine is 87% protein and contains no sugar. (The brands already flavored are 85% sugar.)
- Be sure to follow the diet — your reward will be well worth the effort.

Maintenance Diet

By the time you have completed your 14-day diet, you will have noted the advantages of the change in your eating habits. You can keep your weight at the level you want it — at which you feel and look the best — by continuing to keep your intake of fats, starches, and sugars low and by not over-eating.

In analyzing the eating habits of people who have a tendency to become overweight, it has been found that in practically all cases it is a matter of over-eating and poor eating habits. In approximately 98% of the cases that have come under our observation, most overweight people eat more than they should. In many cases, these people do not even realize this is so.

The surplus of intake, many times, does not take place at the table — but in the preparation of the food. Every time you taste food that is being cooked, you are adding to your intake.

Many women, also, in clearing the table after the meal is over, will eat bits of food that are left. There is not enough to put in the refrigerator — and it seems extravagant to throw it away. So they will eat it. Even if it is only a small fragment, it is better to put it away until lunch the next day or even throw it away than use it to add surplus weight.

Another pitfall to the overweight person is the food offered in another person's home. Your hostess takes pride in preparing especially delicious food for you and it is usually rich in calories. The only way to handle this problem during your diet is to explain that you are on a diet and cannot deviate from it. Or else it is better to decline invitations for two weeks than to lose the benefits of the diet.

After the two weeks' diet is completed, when visiting, you can limit yourself to the minimum amount of food you can accept and still show appreciation for your hostess' hospitality. If, in spite of this, you feel you ate too much, cut down on your diet the next day at home — omitting fats, starches and sugars for a few days — until you have lost the weight gained in the break of your maintenance diet.

The following foods are low in calories and can be used freely in your maintenance diet:

Upon arising — 8-ounce glass of warm water with juice of 1/2 lemon.

Juices: Apple, carrot, celery, beet, grape, etc. Lemon juice (not more than 1/2 lemon in 8-ounce glass of water).

Soups: Clear broth, thin soups such as vegetable, etc. Avoid creamed or thickened soups.

Meat: Lean meat — beef, lamb, veal, liver, heart, kidney, chicken, turkey, fish, other than salmon, tuna, sardines, or any preserved in oil. *Do not fry meat or fish.*

Egg: Boiled four minutes, poached, or hard boiled. *Do not fry.* Omelettes or souffles should be baked. Do not add butter.

Vegetables: Serve green leafy and yellow vegetables every day. Carrots, squash, green string beans, spinach, broccoli, beet tops, kale, cucumbers, artichokes, watercress, zucchini, celery, asparagus, turnip tops, dandelion greens, parsley, lettuce, tomatoes, endive. These vegetables can be used cooked, some raw, some in juices.

Fruits: Apples, grapes, pear, oranges, grapefruit, fresh pineapple, etc.

Milk: Skimmed milk and butter-milk, yogurt.

Bread: Whole grain only — preferably toasted — limit 1 to 2 slices per day.

Butter: Limit yourself to not more than two squares a day. Unsalted.

Cereals: Whole grain cereals in moderate quantities with skimmed milk.

Wheat Germ: Wheat germ can be added to cereals and sprinkled over salads. Three to four tablespoonfuls a day will give you an excellent source of the B vitamins and vitamin E.

Desserts: Apple sauce or baked apple without sugar. Add cinnamon for flavor if desired. Prunes without sugar. Stew until tender and let stand to sweeten with natural sugar. Prune whip with egg-white, no sugar. fresh fruits, berries, etc., without sugar.

Fresh fruits and fruit juices will supply ample natural sugar for your needs. If you eat enough of these, you will not crave sweets.

Salt & Condiments: Do not add salt or other condiments. The moderate use of a vegetable salt in cooking is sufficient for your needs.

Water: Drink an average of about eight glasses of liquids a day. This should include water, fresh juices, fruit and vegetable juice, herb tea, etc.